Power Networking

Using the Contacts You Don't Even Know You Have to Succeed in the Job You Want

Marc Kramer

VGM Career Horizons
NTC/Contemporary Publishing Company

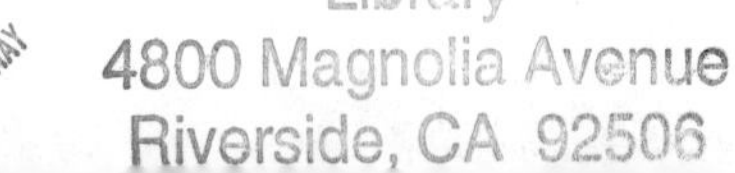

ication Data

Kramer, Marc.

Power networking : using the contacts you don't even know you have to succeed in the job you want / Marc Kramer.

p. cm.

ISBN 0-8442-4494-5

1. Job hunting. 2. Career changes. 3. Career development. 4. Social networks. I. Title.

HF5382.7.K68 1997

650.14—dc21 97-15770

CIP

Cover design by Monica Baziuk

Interior design by Mary Lockwood

Published by VGM Career Horizons

An imprint of NTC/Contemporary Publishing Company

4255 West Touhy Avenue, Lincolnwood (Chicago), Illinois 60646-1975 U.S.A.

Manufactured in the United States of America

International Standard Book Number: 0-8442-4494-5

18 17 16 15 14 13 12 11 10 9 8 7 6 5 4 3 2 1

Contents

Acknowledgments vii

1 Ten Keys to Being a Great Networker 1

Dress Appropriately and Get to Events Early 4
Bring Plenty of Business Cards 5
Mentally Make a Goal to Meet Five New People in an Hour 6
Never Start a Conversation by Talking About Yourself 7
When Talking About Your Company, Make Your Explanation Short 7
Keep Your Conversations Short and Focused 8
Never Sit With Colleagues from Your Own Company at an Event 9
Never Sit With a Friend at an Event 10
Never Talk About Sports, Weather, or Entertainment at an Event 11
Always Send a Letter Within Two Business Days Following a Meeting to the People You Want to Know 11

2 Networking to Find the Right Job 13

How I Developed My Career by Networking 14
Who to Contact 18
What to Say to Build Your Job-Finding Network 37
How to Follow Up Your Contacts 39
How to Shine in Job Interviews 39

3 Networking to Increase Sales 47
Five Keys to Successful Sales Networking 48
Who to Contact 52
What to Say to Build Your Sales Network 54
What to Avoid Discussing 55
Going the Extra Mile 56
Appropriate Information to Provide 58
4 Networking to Raise Money 63
Who to Contact 65
What to Say When Meeting Potential Investors 69
What to Do After Your Initial Meeting with Potential Investors 72
Appropriate Information to Provide 72
5 Writing Good Introductory and Follow-Up Letters 75
Keys to Writing a Good Letter 76
Letters to Potential Employers 77
Letters for Prospective Clients 87
6 Maintaining Networking Relationships 93
Maintain Integrity 95
Give Appropriate Gifts 97
Hosting Business Associates at Home 99
Inviting Business Associates to Events 100

7 Networking at Different Corporate Levels 103

Choosing Appropriate Contacts 104
Finding Information About Potential Contacts 105
Networking for Sales with Everyone Below the Top Executive Offices 108
Networking with Company Presidents 109
Networking with Second-Tier Executives 113

8 Good Networking Organizations 119

Public Organizations 120
Government Entities 123
Private Nonprofit Organizations 124
Events 127
Trade Associations 129

9 Starting Your Own Networking Organization 135

An Example: The Eastern Technology Council 136
How to Begin 139

10 Networking Through the Internet 143

Chat Groups 144
On-Line Services 145

Postscript 151

Acknowledgments

Writing *Power Networking* has been time-consuming but rewarding. I would like to thank my wife Jackie and my girls, Ariel and Sydney, for their patience and understanding throughout this process. There were many days when they wanted my attention and I was busy, either writing or thinking about what I was going to write. My wife was especially great at explaining to my girls how important this book was for me.

I want to thank my parents, Shelly and Bob, who have always supported me. I would have quit writing long ago if it wasn't for my father's consistent prodding when I first started out. I also want to thank my mother-in-law, Alicia McMahon, who has given me moral support ever since we first met.

A special thanks to my sisters Randi and Leslie, my brothers-in-law Neil and Mike, and my friends Gary Samartino, Rachael Simon, Colin Wahl, and Rob Weber for reading and editing my manuscript and making suggestions about what to include.

It has been a pleasure working with my editor, Betsy Lancefield; I appreciate her confidence in me. A special thanks to Julia Anderson, project editor, for the work she did.

Thank you to all the board members and staff at the Downingtown Marketplace, Penn State Technology Development Center, Eastern Technology Council, Pennsylvania Private Investors Group, and Mixed Media Works for providing me with the opportunities that led to my writing this book.

1

Ten Keys to Being a Great Networker

I came from a small town and my father was a successful small-town merchant. His world of contacts didn't reach further than our hometown, Coatesville, which is 50 miles southwest of Philadelphia. When I graduated from West Virginia University in 1982 with a degree in broadcast journalism, the only people I knew were from my hometown. If I was going to expand my world of opportunities, I needed to increase my business and social contacts.

Over the last ten years, I have been fortunate to win many honors and be asked to sit on many boards. There are several honors I am especially proud of: being named Entrepreneur of the Year by Ernst and Young and *Inc.* magazine; becoming a trustee of the oldest English-speaking theater in the western world, the Walnut Street Theater; and becoming a trustee of the oldest African-American university, Cheyney University. I owe these achievements in large part to what I've learned about being a great networker.

This book was developed because many people have asked me how I got to know so many prominent people, to be invited to join major social boards of directors, and to win so many awards and accolades at such a young age. The key, I tell people, is following that old cliché—"It isn't what you know, it's who you know."

Being a good networker is essential. The ability to successfully network can create job and sales opportunities. This chapter presents the ten keys to being a great networker.

The term *networking* became very chic in the 1980s when titans of industry and Wall Street were meeting at conferences, conventions, and seminars to discuss business deals. Prior to the 1980s, the most successful people were paid for *what* they knew, not *who* they knew. That all changed with the breakdown of the long-term one-company career.

Now employers want to know how extensive an employee's network of contacts is. What can an employee bring to a company besides product or service knowledge or the ability to explain a product or service?

The classified advertisements section of every newspaper is full of job opportunities, but professional job hunters will tell you the best opportunities aren't listed in the newspaper, and eight out of ten times the person who gets the job knows someone at the company. Aren't we all more comfortable with a recommendation from someone about a job candidate, than not knowing anything at all?

Here are the ten keys to being a great networker:

1. Dress appropriately and get to events early.
2. Bring plenty of business cards.
3. Make a goal to meet five new people in an hour.
4. Never start a conversation by talking about yourself.
5. When talking about your company, make your explanation short.
6. Keep your conversations short and focused.
7. Never sit with colleagues from your own company at an event.
8. Never sit with a friend you normally socialize with at an event.
9. Never talk about sports, weather, or entertainment at a business event.
10. Always send a letter to the people you want to know within two business days following a meeting.

Now that you know the ten keys, let's look at each one separately.

Dress Appropriately and Get to Events Early

I hate trite sayings, but unfortunately they often prove to be accurate, like the expression, "You never get a second chance to make a good first impression." When going to a business event it's critical to be dressed appropriately.

When men go to a formal business function, they should wear a quality-made suit, starched shirt, conservative tie, and polished shoes. Women should wear either nice suits or a conservative dress.

Don't buy inexpensive suits. A good suit says a lot about the person in it. If you are going to cut corners, buy a moderately priced car. Most business associates rarely see your car.

Women shouldn't wear any suit, dress, or ensemble that takes away from the verbal messages they are trying to convey. I was once at a presentation being made by a very attractive woman who was looking for investors for her company. She had undergraduate and masters degrees in business administration from a prestigious school, but all any of the mostly male audience could remember about her presentation was the provocative blouse she was wearing. No matter how liberal, forward-thinking, and accepting of women in the workplace men have become, we unfortunately lose focus easily.

If you are going to a semiformal function, buy nice casual clothes. It's important to look well-groomed because that makes a statement about who you are and how you picture yourself. A man should wear a nice sweater or sports coat with casual slacks; a woman should wear a nice blouse or sweater and casual slacks.

Once you are dressed and ready to go, it's important to be at a function early. This is because the number one reason you go to any function is not to hear the speaker, but to meet new people. If you arrive early, you can meet, greet, establish relationships, and give out business cards.

In the fall of 1989, I attended a dinner, and before the dinner I got to chatting with a very prominent person in the technology business community. He invited me to join him for dinner, and during the meal, I told him I was bored with my current position and was looking for a new opportunity. He offered me a job on his staff, which I politely declined, and he told me about a new organization that was looking for an executive director.

This organization, known today as the Eastern Technology Council, hired me four months later as its first executive director and provided me with a platform to be on the cover of two magazines and win industry awards. It also readied me to be president of a technology company. This is just one of many examples of how arriving early to an event to network can pay off.

Bring Plenty of Business Cards

Business cards are more important than brochures or any other form of promotion. A good business card should have the usual information, including your e-mail address. Carry a special business card case with at least ten business cards at all times. Also, keep extra business cards in your wallet, briefcase and car—you never know when you will meet a good contact.

My wife and I were on an international flight. During flights I generally divide my time between reading and striking up a conversation with the people around me. Quite by happenstance, on this particular flight, I discovered the passenger sitting next to me on the plane was the regional manager of a software company my association was trying to recruit. At the end of the flight, I gave her my card, wrote down her address and telephone number, and immediately sent a fax back to my office requesting they contact her.

Another time, I was waiting in line at a parking garage for my car when I struck up a conversation with a gentleman who was president of a company my organization had been trying to connect with for two years. Because we were in an informal situation, he was receptive to talking with me at long last and furthermore was receptive when I asked him to exchange business cards. A month later I visited his office and got him to join our organization.

Mentally Make a Goal to Meet Five New People in an Hour

Too many times people attend events and spend their whole evening speaking to one person. It's very hard to build a network if you spend all of your time at every event meeting just one new person. The individual—whose time you may be dominating—may wish to meet other people. You need to be considerate of why people come to events.

I try to meet a new person every 5 to 10 minutes. My goal is to make five new introductions and bring home my new contacts' business cards so I can write to them and set up a second meeting if I feel it's warranted.

Never Start a Conversation by Talking About Yourself

Many professionals are guilty of trying to sell everyone they meet on their company or firm. True, the idea of networking is primarily to pick up business contacts, but networking is like dating. People usually don't like someone to come up to them and start talking about him- or herself. I think the reason people make this mistake is because they are nervous and aren't sure what to say.

I have several approaches when speaking with people I don't know.

1. If I don't know anything about their company, I will ask them for a brief explanation of who they are and what they do.
2. If I know something about their company or industry, I will ask them for their opinion on a particular topic.
3. If I know someone in their company, I will ask them if they know the person. If they say no, I will ask them what department they work in.

Once I hear about the person's job and company, I will mention what I do. If I think the company is an appropriate target, I will ask who in the company I should write to and speak with.

When Talking About Your Company, Make Your Explanation Short

All too often people feel compelled to tell their whole life story and everything about their company. But networking opportunities are like sound bites. The purpose is to get the person with whom you are speaking interested in what you can do for him or her, so the contact will want to have a second meeting. The following is an example of what you should say after finding out briefly about the other person:

> "I am a lawyer with Smith and Jones. We are a patent firm specializing in software companies. You may have heard of some of our clients: Gates Software, Veins Interactive, and Mixed Media."

In less than a minute the person knows what you do, the name of your firm, your firm's specialty, and client references. If you are interested in meeting with this person, the conversation should end as follows:

> "I enjoyed meeting you and I don't want to hold you up from meeting other people. Why don't we get together and have you come to our offices for lunch. Here is my business card. I will call within the week to set a date. It was great meeting you."

Keep Your Conversations Short and Focused

It's easy to get off track speaking for any length of time. Remember why you are at an event—to make contacts and qualify potential business. Don't start the conversation off by talking about any of the following, which I will discuss in greater detail later:

- Weather
- Sports
- Quality of the food
- Political news
- Comments you heard on the car radio on the way to the event

Try to avoid the temptation of talking about yourself. Instead ask direct questions that will allow you to ascertain whether or not you want to have a second meeting with this person. You should ask the following questions:

- What does your company do?
- How large is your company?
- Who are some of your well-known clients?
- What is your position in the company?

After those questions are answered you should tell the person what you and your firm do. Provide the person with a business card and then, if he or she is the appropriate person in the organization you want to meet with, tell him or her you will call for an appointment. If your contact isn't the appropriate person, ask for an introduction or for permission to use the person's name when contacting one of his or her colleagues.

Never Sit with Colleagues from Your Own Company at an Event

We all probably see our coworkers more than our own families, because we spend so much time at the office. When going to an event, seminar, or semibusiness function, sitting with coworkers isn't going to widen your network. All too often companies buy tables at events and end up having their employees sit with people they see every day.

When the trade association I worked with hosted events and guests had to purchase table seating in advance, I would suggest to the companies that they buy a table's worth of seats, but that the seats be spread out among different tables. People were usually cool to this idea because they generally don't feel comfortable sitting next to strangers. They worry about what they will talk about.

I told the people purchasing the table that they were doing a disservice to themselves and their company by encouraging their employees to sit together. Whenever my organization attended someone else's function, I would request they split us up. At our own events, it was a given you sat with people you didn't know.

Once companies listened to and followed this advice, they found the results so beneficial that thereafter they never allowed their people to sit together again.

Never Sit with a Friend at an Event

We are all comfortable with and look forward to seeing close friends. A lot of the friends whom my wife and I socialize with run companies. Every time I see them they ask me if I would like to sit with them. I politely decline and explain that events are work to me. My job is to meet as many new people as possible and make quality business contacts. Once I explain that going to events is work for me, their feelings aren't hurt because they understand how fruitful this approach is for me.

Never Talk About Sports, Weather, or Entertainment at an Event

Because most of us are uncomfortable speaking with strangers, we usually try to start off with a safe topic like the weather, the local sports team, or the newest exhibit at the art museum. I consider this wasting valuable time. Most successful business executives I have met enjoy reading biographies, which to me means they like finding out about people, businesses, and what makes them work.

Think of every new person you meet at a business function as a living biography. Wouldn't you rather find out what that person and his or her company does and what is happening in his or her industry than talk about something you can read in the newspaper?

There is an appropriate time to talk about sports and entertainment—when you are having a one-on-one breakfast, lunch, or dinner meeting, or perhaps when playing a game of golf. That information can be helpful for developing a rapport with someone. People enjoy working with others who share their leisure interests and hobbies.

Always Send a Letter Within Two Business Days Following a Meeting to the People You Want to Know

Don't wait a week to contact someone you just met who could potentially do something positive for you. People who do a lot of networking may not remember who you are more than two days after your initial meeting. This is especially true when meeting people at a large dinner, seminar, or major event.

I always do one of two things when reconnecting with someone I meet. I either send a short one-to-three-paragraph fax with some information about my company, or I send a letter with our brochure. Later in the book are sample follow-up letters that you can use as a guide.

2

Networking to Find the Right Job

No matter where you live in the world, finding the right opportunity hinges more on who you know than what you know. My experience, outlined in the following section, illustrates how networking can be used to advance a career.

How I Developed My Career by Networking

When I graduated college I knew no one outside of the small town in which I grew up. My father had and still operates a small medical equipment business on the main street. If my life's ambition was to stay and work in my hometown, my father knew practically all of the other small business owners.

I graduated with a journalism degree from West Virginia in May of 1982. It was a bad year to be coming out of college with a journalism degree because ten major newspapers folded, including our beloved *Philadelphia Bulletin,* the largest evening daily newspaper in the country. When I graduated, only 10 percent of the journalism students were able to get jobs in the field.

Fortunately, my father knew someone who had just started a weekly free newspaper called the *Village News.* I met the publisher, who was also the president of the company, top salesperson, and part-time delivery person. After a short interview, I was hired as the sports editor for $60 a week. Within a couple of weeks, I was making $120 a week and writing 16 stories per week.

I appreciated my father making the introduction, but I knew I had to do something on my own if I was going to make enough money to move out of my parents' house. I asked the editor of the paper if I could start covering the Rotary and chamber of commerce functions, along with my sports beat. This, I thought, would be a good way for me to meet people, especially the publisher of the town's only daily newspaper, the *Coatesville Record.*

After getting a chance to meet the local publisher at various Rotary and chamber functions, it occurred to me that I could enhance the quality and circulation of the local daily with some creative ideas. I mentioned some of my ideas to the publisher. He listened politely, but didn't take me seriously. The *Coatesville Record* was owned by a chain and so I decided to write the publisher's boss, who headed the chain.

I sent him a business plan with editorial, marketing, and distribution ideas. He was impressed enough to call me and invite me to lunch with the *Record's* publisher. After a nice lunch, they offered me a job as a reporter for the daily at $200 a week. Within eight months of graduation, I had tripled my salary.

After a year in this position I was laid off. I needed to make more money because I was getting married, so I began my search for a new career. No one from my immediate circle of family, friends, and contacts knew anything about putting together a proper resume or knew someone I should speak with. The first resume I put together was done on a typewriter and printed on cheap photocopy paper.

I sent this resume to hundreds of companies. The only contact I tried was my mother's brother, a manager for a Big Six accounting firm. I sent him my resume, and he told me no one would respond to a resume that looked so unprofessional. He gave me good advice on how to improve my resume. I rewrote the resume and had it typeset and printed on good paper, and companies started responding more positively. (Today, most people who graduate from college either have a home computer or easy access to one, and many computers have resume-formatting software. There is no excuse for having an unprofessional-looking resume.)

In a couple of months, I went to work for a private company that collected school and municipal taxes. Right after I got this job I married. During the next year, I worked five jobs simultaneously. I taught tennis after work, sold patio furniture for a garden store after dinner, taught tennis for the local YMCA on Saturday mornings and was a youth group advisor on Sundays, and started a side business selling bumper stickers to businesses and nonprofit organizations.

My side business initially went nowhere, so I changed it. I told businesses and nonprofits I could get them anything. Marching bands, professional athletes, bumper stickers, t-shirts, mugs, whatever. This led me to a man who ran the largest indoor small business center in the area. The owner told me he needed a haunted house built in an 800-square-foot store and would pay me the equivalent of 10 percent of my then gross salary for one day's work.

My wife suggested I contact the theater department at her alma mater, West Chester University, and hire theater students to put together and run the haunted house. I obtained sheets from a hotel, dyed them black and strung them on wires, and hung inexpensive Halloween ornaments. The evening was a grand success.

At the end of the evening the owner fired his assistant and hired me. For almost two years I worked for this gentleman until he ran into financial trouble. Again, I was put in the awkward position of having to look for another job. I had the same problem as before—no contacts.

I saw an advertisement in the *Philadelphia Inquirer* for a manager for a business incubator that Penn State University was launching at one of its suburban campuses. A business incubator assists start-up companies by providing inexpensive office space, shared secretarial services and business equipment, and experienced business executives for advice and consultation.

I applied for the position. Dr. Lawrence Cote, center executive officer of the campus, hired me after one interview. The key to the success of my interview was that I provided a vision for the incubator and never asked about the salary. I felt if I received the offer, then I could decide if the salary was satisfactory. Dr. Cote told me I was the only candidate to have a vision and not ask about the money.

This position was very important in launching my professional managerial career. I realized that if I didn't want to repeat the problems I had when I left my last job, it was important to develop a network of contacts. I had learned that the two most important weapons for moving ahead are knowledge and contacts. In most white-collar professional positions, it isn't enough just to be knowledgeable. Having a strong business network to open doors is just as essential.

Over the past ten years, many top executives have sent me their resumes, knocked on my door, and asked me who they should meet with. In the beginning these inquiries would surprise me, because these people were presidents, executive vice presidents, and chief financial officers. I assumed, because of the level of their positions, they knew people from other companies, business organizations, and so forth. But I discovered that what happens all too often, especially with people in large corporations, is that they become wrapped up in their own company's world. They never think they will be looking outside the company for a job and so they don't develop outside contacts.

It is rare today that someone spends an entire career working for one company. Most people change jobs at least five to seven times during the course of a career. I personally have been with seven different organizations over the last fourteen years—and thanks in part to networking, all of my moves have been upward.

You can't plan on being with a company a long time. Many employers look for people who have had diverse experiences with a variety of companies. Companies believe that diversity makes for a better, more productive employee—an employee who brings new ideas and energy to the job.

There are two questions everyone who is networking for a job asks me: who to contact, and what to say. These questions are answered in the following sections.

Who to Contact

Most people have a large network of contacts, but tend to overlook them. People forget that their parents, siblings, spouses, neighbors, recreational sports teammates, country club, bridge group, and Boy Scout troop parents are all potential contacts for employment and sales opportunities.

The following is a list of thirteen resources that can provide new employment opportunities.

Personal Friends in Other Companies

Don't be bashful or think you are imposing by calling a friend when you are looking for a new opportunity. If you are a quality professional, you can be doing your friend and his or her company a favor by letting them know you are available. Personal friends are good resources because they already think highly of you and are willing to do whatever they can to help. Also, friends may be able to call suppliers and clients to open up opportunities.

Business Peers in Other Companies

Sooner or later you are going to meet your competition, and, if you make the right impression, your competition can be your best ally in the future. Because we are in such a competitive environment, businesses look at competitors as a good source of potential employees. After meeting a competitor, it never hurts to send a note acknowledging that you met and offering future assistance if needed. Because my company cultivates such relationships, recently a competitor contacted us asking if we wanted to collaborate on a project that required two companies to handle it.

Former Managers Who Have Moved On

Always stay in touch with managers you respected when they move on to other companies. That former manager may have an opportunity or know of an opportunity that you would like.

Headhunters

Headhunters are human resource professionals who assist companies in finding the right person for a particular position in an organization. Most headhunters have either an industry specialty or a position specialty and in some cases both. Headhunters are probably the ultimate networkers, because they rely on their networks to find quality candidates for their clients.

Once you get to know a headhunter, it is a good idea to keep him or her updated on what you are doing. You never know when a headhunter will call you with a position you may be attracted to. It's also good to keep in touch with a headhunter in the event you lose your job and need to find another one.

Avoid headhunters who want to either charge a fee for their services or require partial payment for their services.

Don't hesitate to ask headhunters for recommendations of other professionals in their field or organizations they deal with. You always want to enlarge your network of contacts.

Career Centers

Career centers assist professionals in deciding a strategy for developing their careers. These organizations usually employ both job counselors and employment specialists. Job counselors assist people in deciding what career would be most appropriate based on the person's interests and skills. Employment specialists have lists of job opportunities provided by regional companies.

Career centers are usually good places to go if you want to make a career change or aren't sure of your professional direction. The employment opportunities usually found are low-level management and entry-level positions.

Employment Agencies

There are three types of employment agencies. One type of agency develops a relationship with a business that requires the new hire to pay the job search fee. The second type receives a retainer and search completion fee from the company that engaged them to find employees. Most employment agencies fall into the third category, which is a blend of the first two: the fee is divided between the new hire and the employer.

Quality opportunities are usually found at agencies who both specialize in a particular area and are compensated by the companies that engage them in the search. Employment agencies can be found in the telephone book. To find out which agencies are best, call the human resource departments of the companies you are either most interested in or you admire. These companies probably have done reference checks on the agencies, and they can let you know which ones they like to work with.

State Unemployment Office

Most people never think of going to the state unemployment office for anything but filing and collecting for unemployment. Unemployment offices usually are connected to a statewide job bank database that sorts by industry and position. Many companies avail themselves of this free service, because the state doesn't charge a finder's fee and professionals who have been laid off usually go to this agency first to sign up for unemployment benefits.

State unemployment offices also have job counselors who are aware of employment opportunities. These counselors are more than glad to help a job seeker scan the state database for employment opportunities. Most of the jobs in this database are entry level, but there are occasional management opportunities on the system.

I found my first nonjournalism job through our local state unemployment office. I had been laid off from my job at our local newspaper and I signed up for unemployment. The unemployment officer took a look at my background and arranged for me to send my resume to and interview with a tax administration and collection company called Berkheimer Associates. I went on one interview and got a job offer that I accepted. I stayed with Berkheimer for a wonderful year and a half.

The Internet

The Internet is the first truly global marketplace that you can access from your home. It is the best and quickest way to search for opportunities and meet new people. More than 80 million people throughout the world have Internet access.

Employment opportunities can be unearthed by using search engines such as AltaVista or Yahoo. Search engines assist users in finding whatever information they are looking for. For example, if you search on the phrase "employment opportunities on the Internet" using AltaVista, you will find 200,000 employment-related sites. There are four types of searches that can provide new opportunities.

Company Searches

By the time you read this book, almost every company in the Fortune 1000 will have a website, and most websites will post job opportunities. Most companies are looking for quality professionals with up-to-date skills, and companies theorize those people probably have home computers and Internet access.

Company websites usually feature an employment opportunities section. This section tells the reader what positions are available and describes the requirements applicants need to be considered. These same sites offer the ability to electronically mail (e-mail) the applicant's resume to the company or fill out a form that goes directly into the company database. Companies are even putting personality tests on-line to see if the candidate fits both the job and the company's culture.

What makes this mechanism better than traditional mail is that people who have used e-mail are in the habit of reading whatever is sent to them, and the sorting systems save both the applicant and the company time.

Below are samples of company websites both large and small:

ibm.com. IBM has a very rich and detailed employment site. The employment section allows the user to search in a variety of ways such as by country, position, openings, greatest needs, and so on.

iscg.com. Integrated Consulting Group (ISCG) is a $30 million in sales publicly traded systems integrator focused on the pharmaceutical industry. ISCG has a subsection dedicated to filling its employment needs, with full job descriptions and a place to fill out your own pertinent information in order to apply for a job with ISCG.

right.com. This is the site for Right Associates, a publicly traded company that provides outplacement and human resources consulting. Right's site shows job opportunities that are available at Right's clients.

Resume Services

Many on-line job services are offered on the Internet. They usually fit one of four categories:

- All industries nationally
- Industry specific nationally
- All industries in a region, state, or country
- Industry specific by region, state or country

These services either have the job seeker pay for the privilege of being on the service or the company pay for access to the service. The services that companies access have a built-in search engine that allows companies to search by college, degree, year of graduation, knowledge base, and professional experiences.

Below are samples of resume services:

asae.org/jobs/. The American Society of Association Executives developed this site. Almost 200 different employment site links are found on this site. They range from companies to colleges/universities to headhunters.

careerbuilder.com. Created by Netstart, this site provides employer postings, allows users to post their resumes, has the ability to search for job opportunities in cities across the country, and provides career advice.

careermosaic.com. This is one of the most comprehensive employment sites on the Internet. It connects to thousands of companies that are looking to fill positions. The site allows users to put their resumes into the system and will even assist the user in developing a resume. Users may also participate in on-line job fairs.

ipa.com. This site was put together by the Internet Professional Association and has received many awards. The site provides a listing of recruiters as well as job listings, allows users to post their resumes, and gives a list of other resources related to finding employment.

smartindia.com. If you are looking overseas and want to get an idea of what jobs are available in another country, take a look at this site. It provides job postings and links to corporate sites all over India.

Job Bulletin Boards

Job bulletin board services show what opportunities are available by profession, industry, position, and region. Here are some examples:

bradson.com. Created by Bradford Staffing Services, a job placement firm, this is a free job bulletin board that provides mostly technical opportunities, but some administrative, sales, and marketing opportunities are posted as well.

npa.org. The Network Professional Association provides job listings and a place for people to post their resumes. Ninety-nine percent of the jobs are technical in nature.

sundaypaper.com. Created by Bulkin Enterprises, this site allows you to search through Sunday newspaper help wanted ads throughout the country and to post your resume for employers to see.

Job Databases

Job database services do searches on the Web for job opportunities.

careerpath.com. Career Path is a national interactive employment service that includes the *Boston Globe, Chicago Tribune, Los Angeles Times, The New York Times,* and other major newspapers. Its databases can be sorted by region, industry, and position.

tv.jobnet.com. America's TV Job Network created this site, which has won many awards. The site contains employment news, career training, a job database and resume databases.

Bestjobsusa.com. *Employment Review* magazine and *USA Today* put this site together. It contains opportunities for all job levels, company sizes, and professions.

What makes the Internet great is its global reach and ability to connect people quickly at all hours of the day and night. For more information on using the Internet to find a job, see *The Guide to Internet Job Searching,* copublished by the Public Library Association and VGM Career Horizons.

Business Organizations

Many business professionals, once they reach a certain status in their corporation, believe they don't need an outside network. They believe their skills alone will be enough to keep them moving up the corporate ladder. They may sneer at the thought of joining business organizations and think them a waste of time and money. Often it was these same individuals who would knock on my door when I was running a trade association, asking me for introductions when they lost their jobs. They knew no one and were no better off than a recent college graduate. It can't be stressed enough how important it is to join business organizations, because the people you meet may know someone or have an opportunity that is just right for you.

There are three types of business organizations I recommend everyone join: trade associations, chambers of commerce, and business clubs.

Trade Associations

Trade associations bring together professionals who are either in the same industry or sell to that industry. There is no better place to network for business leads and job opportunities than a trade association, and nearly every industry has one.

Trade associations provide innumerable networking and visibility opportunities. These opportunities present themselves in the following forms:

- Seminars
- Breakfasts, luncheons, and dinners
- Roundtable discussions
- Committee meetings
- Conventions
- Social outings

The contacts you make at a trade association can last a lifetime. Many of the successful executives I know have developed relationships with professionals in other companies that have led to new opportunities.

Chambers of Commerce

Chambers of commerce offer the same types of events as trade associations, except they aren't industry specific. All chambers are not the same. In my opinion there are two classifications—big city chambers of commerce and all other chambers.

Big City Chambers of Commerce. Big city chambers receive financial and board-of-directors support from large companies, but are usually populated by service providers such as insurance, real estate, and business brokers. Business executives in major cities rarely attend anything except the chamber's annual dinner.

Executives of non-service companies sometimes think of service providers as leeches who don't provide any real value. I completely disagree. Successful service providers have a large network of clients. The best way to network with service providers is to ask them who they serve and whether they can make an introduction.

Small Town and Suburban Chambers of Commerce. You usually can find all of the movers and shakers at midsize and small city or town chamber of commerce functions. Chambers are the best form of networking for business people outside of a major metropolitan area. The local chamber of commerce is usually the area's driving political and economic force. In small towns, if you aren't a member of the chamber, you won't develop a successful network.

Junior Chamber of Commerce. The Jaycees, as this organization is called, can be found in towns and cities across the country. It is made up of young business leaders who are looking to enlarge their network of business contacts and make a difference in society. This organization raises money for education and other charitable causes. Most Jaycees are looking for people to take leadership roles, which will enhance your visibility.

The key to leveraging your membership in a chamber is to get on the board, join committees, and speak at seminars. Once you get involved and people begin to know you, then you are all but assured of being a success. Just make sure you are accessible and accommodating, and that you keep your word. All too often people volunteer and never follow through, which harms both their reputations and their careers.

Business Clubs

There are a few types of business clubs that fall outside of chambers and associations that can be worth joining in order to increase your network. These include breakfast clubs and private investor clubs.

Breakfast Clubs. These are usually made up of eight to ten people, each representing, but not duplicating, a particular profession or industry. The sole purpose of these clubs is to trade business leads and contacts.

Private Investor Clubs. These are groups that bring together past and current presidents and high-level executives from all types of industries. Most clubs require that an individual be an accredited investor, which means the person has $1 million net worth or $250,000 in disposable income. Occasionally these groups will allow nonaccredited individuals to attend their meetings so they might meet a company that can use their skills.

Nonprofit Organizations

Nonprofit organizations are important to the vitality and survival of any region. Today most nonprofits know there is a quid pro quo for people taking time out of their days to get involved. Professionals join nonprofit boards because they are interested in the organization itself as well as in the other people who are sitting on the board. I have served on many boards, and the contacts I have made on these boards have brought me new business and employment opportunities.

I started an organization called the Pennsylvania Private Investors Group, which brings together accredited investors on a monthly basis to meet and listen to companies who are looking for venture capital. Through running this organization, I met a very successful entrepreneur named Herb Cohen, who started the country's largest disc jockey organization—the Pros—which provided entertainment at weddings, bar and bat mitzvahs, and other occasions. Herb liked my entrepreneurial style and, when I left the Eastern Technology Council, suggested to the founder of Mixed Media Works that he hire me as president and chief operating officer. As of the writing of this book, I am still president of this company.

There are three types of nonprofit "power" boards: the arts, charitable causes and foundations, and educational institutions.

Arts Organizations

The theater, orchestra, and ballet are organizations that require corporate and wealthy individual donations and participation. Corporations that support the arts usually have one of their top executives sit on the board of the organization. The level of executive serving on a board depends on the company's financial level of commitment and who else is sitting on that board.

For example, in Philadelphia, the Philadelphia Orchestra's board is the most prestigious. The board is made up of the Philadelphia region's top executives and moneyed society. The cost to join that board is in the range of an upscale country club, and that is just the beginning of the financial commitment. For entrepreneurs and high-level executives who have just begun to make serious money, getting on these types of boards will open doors and provide entree to the powers of politics and business.

In New York, the Metropolitan Museum of Art attracts the most powerful and influential people in New York City. The powers of investment banking, government, and industry are represented. Most of the names on the board are people you read about in *Time*, *The Wall Street Journal*, and *Business Week*.

Charitable Causes and Foundations

The list of worthwhile charitable causes could fill this book. Just about anyone who has stature has some cause he or she is passionate about or feels his or her company should support. The local United Way and Boy/Girl Scout boards provide a wealth of contacts.

The great thing about charitable organizations is that they need both board and committee members. If you can't get on the board of directors, volunteer for a committee, work your way up to chairperson and then, by showing the organization your value, you can try to get on the main board.

Educational Institutions

Educational institutions such as colleges and universities, private school boards, and libraries all attract leading citizens who have influence and power.

Colleges and Universities. The prestige of the school determines how difficult it is to get on the board of trustees. With private institutions it's usually a matter of how much money you can donate. With large public institutions it's any or all of the following—ability to donate large sums of money, political contacts, and ability to get on the alumni ballot, if that is how the school's trustees are elected.

To get on the board of a small to midsize public college, you may be elected as an alumnus of the university, but in most cases you are asked to be a trustee because you are interested in the particular institution and you have strong political connections. Most state system university trustees are appointed by the governor's office. The nomination usually comes through the local legislator's office.

Private School Boards. Most private school boards are made up of either alumni or parents of students. Because private schools are usually so expensive, you usually rub shoulders with titans of business and old money. Like public and private colleges, private schools are always trying to raise money for scholarships and improving the school's facilities. Therefore, you either have to bring money or have the ability to attract people with money who have interest in helping the school.

Libraries. Large inner-city library boards are populated with corporate leaders and high-level executives. These people either feel personally compelled to get involved to make a difference in inner-city education or their companies feel it is important to be a good corporate citizen. It's hard to get on these boards unless you have stature in the community. You usually can get on the mailing list for major fund-raising events, however, and these events provide good opportunities to make quality contacts.

Small and mid-sized libraries usually are looking for good board members who either care about education, bring contacts to raise money, or can donate themselves. These boards usually are made up of small to mid-sized business owners and average citizens. If you get involved in fund-raisers and show a strong interest in improving the library, you can get the head librarian or chairman of the board to nominate you to the board.

Current and Past Clients

Probably the best source of contacts is current and past clients. There are several reasons why this group is a terrific resource.

- They are usually in your professional field, so they know other people you can network with to either find a job or increase your customer list.
- They may want to hire you if they know you are available.
- They are good references, provided you have done quality work for them. (You would be surprised at the occasional professional who asks me to be a reference or uses me as a reference without asking—often when I don't know him or her or didn't think highly enough of the person's work to give a reference.)

One of the best investments one can make is buying a home computer that has software to track contacts. If you already have a computer, buy contact software. Once you have set up your contact list, keep it current. It can be a bit time-consuming, but is worth the investment.

One way to stay in touch with current or past clients is to send them congratulatory letters, faxes, or e-mails for:

A new promotion. A sample body of the letter/e-mail is:

> Congratulations concerning your new promotion to vice president of marketing. Let's get together for breakfast or lunch so you can fill me in on your duties and let me

> know how I can help you. I will call you in the next week to set a date.

A big sale you heard the client made. A sample body of the letter/e-mail is:

> I read in the Business Journal you just landed a multimillion-dollar sale to Smith Company. That's quite a coup. Let's get together for breakfast or lunch so you can get me up to speed on your company. I will call you next week to set a date.

Another method for staying in touch, if you have a hobby in common, is to inform the client of something related to the hobby. A sample body of a letter/e-mail is:

> Last week I was at the Civil War Buff Association's annual meeting and I didn't see you. Are you still collecting Civil War memorabilia? I bought an old Confederate flag you might like to see.
>
> I was hoping to see you at the meeting, so we could catch up. I will call your office to see if you are available for breakfast or lunch. Look forward to seeing you soon.

Or

> I saw this article about your favorite Civil War general, Stonewall Jackson, and thought you would enjoy it. I hope all is going well. Let's get together for breakfast or lunch to get caught up. I will call you in the next week. Take care.

You can let current or old clients know that you have changed jobs, are looking to change jobs, or are seeking their help because you have left your current position. A sample body of the letter/e-mail is:

> I don't know if you heard yet, but I have left Jones Company and I am looking for a new opportunity. Maybe we could get together for breakfast or lunch to fill you in on what I am looking for. Enclosed is my resume. I will call your office to set a date.

My recommendation for people who have lost their jobs and plan to send letters to past and current customers is to present themselves as a business consultant, not someone looking for a job. Send a cover letter telling your contact you have just left your most recent employer and have decided to do some consulting, while looking for other opportunities. Printing business cards and developing an at-home consulting practice is relatively inexpensive. Providing ideas on how your contacts can improve their business costs only time, but the potential upside could be tremendous.

Seminars

I mentioned the value of seminars in the first chapter, but I feel it's important to remind the reader of a few more important points. When selecting a seminar, look at the list of speakers and ask people in the industry what they think of the group giving the seminar.

Always get to seminars early. The best networking opportunities occur before the seminar, during breaks, and after the seminar. Don't sit with friends at seminars. You are there to meet new people. Remember, one of your goals should be to collect as many business cards as possible and open your network of potential contacts.

College Alumni Associations

College alumni associations are a terrific source for networking, especially if the college is in your local area. In Pennsylvania, for example, if you are a graduate of Penn State University the doors open quickly and often. If you graduated from West Virginia University, like myself, and went to work in Philadelphia, your university affiliation doesn't carry the same weight.

I would encourage high school seniors and recent college graduates who are thinking of going to graduate school to think about where they might like to live after college or plan to make their home. If you go to an elite school like the University of Pennsylvania's Wharton School of Business or Stanford University, doors will open regardless of your location because of the prestige of the schools.

What's great about going to a prestigious school is that many top executives come from these schools. If you look at the list of top executives in the Fortune 500, most of them went to highly respected academic schools. People who graduate from top schools feel an affinity and have a respect for people who went to schools with a similar standing.

If you don't go to an elite school, try to attend your state's leading state-supported university. Once you've graduated, get involved with the alumni association. Alumni associations are powerful bonding clubs. These groups go to sporting events together, host golf tournaments and alumni receptions. Many people forget the alumni association can be a great door opener. Join your local alumni association, get the alumni directory and use it.

What to Say to Build Your Job-Finding Network

In order for your contacts to help you build your career, you must keep the conversation on target. Other subjects, unless related to your networking opportunity, will not provide insight to what this new contact has to offer. Save that conversation for small talk before you have a meal with this new contact.

Don't immediately launch into a monologue of who you are and why you are there. Stay away from telling someone you are looking for a new opportunity.

When going over to a complete stranger, just say the following:

YOU: Hi! I am Marc Kramer.

Their reply will be to say "I am Jane Smith." The rest of the conversation should go as follows:

YOU: Jane, what company are you with?

RESPONSE: I am with Smith Company.

YOU: What does your company do?

SMITH: We are systems integrators.

YOU: Who do you sell to?

SMITH: We sell strictly to the pharmaceutical market.

YOU: That's a market with a lot of money. What do you do for your company?

SMITH: I am a sales manager.

As your conversation progresses ask yourself the following questions:

- Do I want or can I get business from this person's company?
- Is this the appropriate person in Smith Company to speak with? If not, I need to ask her to make an introduction.
- What can I bring to the table that would interest her in my company or skill set?

Once you have determined whether you want to do business with Ms. Smith's company and Ms. Smith, you should proceed to tell her about your consulting practice. Below are three ways to continue the conversation:

> YOU: I have done a lot of work over the past three years with pharmaceutical companies such as SmithKline, Wyeth Ayerst, and Glaxo. Maybe we should get together at your office sometime in the next week or so. Please give me your business card, and here is mine. I will call you.

> YOU: I have done some work with pharmaceutical companies in the area of reengineering consulting. Maybe there is something we can do together. Here is my card, and why don't you give me yours. I will call you to set up an appointment, if that is okay with you.

> YOU: From what you described, it sounds as if our two companies should be doing business together. Who would be the appropriate person for me to contact? Here are two of my business cards. Please pass this on to the appropriate person and I will follow up with a call to him or her sometime at the end of next week.

All of the above replies require you to get someone's name and number, and narrow down a date to take the relationship to the next level. It's important to come to agreement on what the next step should be. Never leave this type of conversation open-ended. Nothing will get accomplished. The following section describes how to follow up on the contacts you have made to establish your network.

How to Follow Up Your Contacts

There are two good times to contact people: early in the morning before their secretaries, administrative assistants, and meetings begin, or after 5 or 6 P.M., when everyone has left. Find out early on if the person works early in the morning or late in the evening. It's been my experience that creative people such as software developers and scientists are late-night people. Sales and marketing people usually like to be in early.

Today, I would recommend either faxing or e-mailing correspondence. People usually open traditional mail last, and if they aren't looking for something in particular, they might not open it until the end of the week.

Letters 2.1 and 2.2 are sample letters to send after meeting someone at a seminar. Remember to keep your letter short and to the point. Begin it by reminding the person where you met and why you would like to meet again.

How to Shine in Job Interviews

When meeting people for the first time in a job interview, you have to be thinking about everything you say. You can't let

Letter 2.1

John Smith
Sales Manager
Smith Company
100 Smith Blvd.
Smithville, OH 19999

Dear John,

It was a pleasure meeting you at the Cleveland Business Council's seminar on reengineering the corporation. As I mentioned when we spoke, I would like to speak with you about possibly doing business together.

I think my experience and background can add value to what you are already doing. I will call you in the next couple of days to set up an appointment. Please don't hesitate to call or e-mail me if I can be of assistance to you.

Sincerely,

Marc Kramer
President

Seminar Follow-up

Jane Smith
Sales Manager
Smith Company
100 Smith Blvd.
Smithville, OH 19999

Dear Jane,

It was a pleasure meeting you at the Cleveland Business Council's seminar on reengineering the corporation. As I mentioned when we spoke, I would appreciate an introduction to the appropriate person you feel I should meet with regarding my area of expertise.

I will call you in the next few days. If you don't have time to speak with me, just leave with your secretary the name of the person I should call or fax/e-mail it to me. Your assistance is greatly appreciated. Please don't hesitate if I can be of assistance to you.

Sincerely,

Marc Kramer
President

your mind wander and go on autopilot. Your verbal and body language will determine if you are successful with the individual you are speaking with. It's important to come across as well-spoken and energized. People have respect for individuals who have those two traits.

The verbal language is different for a recent college graduate and a seasoned professional. Let's take a look at each group separately.

College Graduate Job Interviewing

Most people hate going on job interviews. They are afraid of saying something wrong and look at the interviewer as someone sitting in judgment on them. Job interviewing can be fun and intellectually challenging, and it provides one of the best networking opportunities.

Talk about the following:

- What you enjoyed about college, from classes to concerts to sports.
- What you learned in your classes.
- The type of teacher you enjoyed.
- Where the interviewer went to school. He or she may have graduated from the same school as you or someone you know. If you know something about the school and can say something positive, it will make you and the interviewer more comfortable.
- Jobs you had during the school year and in the summer.
- Your personal goals and ambitions.
- How you handled responsibility.

Avoid saying the following:

- Don't talk about what a great partier you were in school. Every interviewer looks for red flags that will allow him or her to eliminate a candidate, so you want to appear to be responsible.
- When asked about your weaknesses, never say you aren't detail oriented, have difficulty being on time, or are more interested in lifestyle than business success. Every employer wants to know you will work extra hours and are well organized.
- If you have been fired from a job, don't blame your boss even if he or she was wrong. Interviewers will say they understand, but they are thinking maybe there is something wrong with you. Talk about what you learned from being fired and what you would have done differently.

Before going on an interview, it is wise to find out about the company's culture. There are cultures that embrace people who are entrepreneurial and there are others that look at entrepreneurs as mavericks who will constantly be at odds with the company's system. Shortly after graduating college, I made the mistake of not finding out about a company's culture before going on an interview, and it cost me what I thought at the time a great opportunity.

Experienced Professional Job Interviewing

Few people ever like interviewing for a position, but most people who have been in the workforce for at least ten years find it easier. The reason is that people are moving from company to company more often. The days of someone spending his or her whole professional life with one company are gone.

I was asked to interview for a sales position with one of the top educational publishers in the country. The position paid a great base salary, terrific benefits, and a generous commission. I thought I would impress the interviewer with my entrepreneurial bent.

I told the interviewer how I started a t-shirt business in college, proceeded by starting a syndicated sports writing service that unfortunately failed, followed by a bumper sticker business, and that my aspiration was to start and own a company someday.

To many people, what I said could be interpreted as indicating that I was highly motivated, ambitious, and a self-starter. The interviewer said he liked my aggressiveness, but didn't think I would be a fit. I asked why and he told me the company didn't want to make an investment in someone who could be leaving in a few years. He went on to tell me that the company believed it took three to five years to recoup its educational investment and looked for employees who wanted to work their way up the corporate ladder.

While college graduates may have a difficult time breaking in because they have no experience, experienced professionals sometimes have a difficult time moving into new opportunities because of financial, geographic, family, and corporate cultural changes. With that said, experienced professionals need to be focused at interviews, so they don't make elimination mistakes in job interviewing.

Talk about the following:

One time I was interviewing someone for a sales position. This person had a wonderful resume, charming personality, and great industry contacts. The only problem I had with this person is that he seemed to have moved from company to company every 18 to 24 months for the past eight years. He went over his history and told me that one boss was disorganized and didn't know what he was doing, another shouldn't have been a manager because she was just incompetent, and the last boss didn't appreciate how hard the person had worked for her.

The warning bell went off in my head. I thought to myself that it might be impossible to make this person happy. Would this person become disenchanted with my organization and speak poorly about us? I felt that this person might have an attitude problem, one that we couldn't afford to try to change.

If this person had said he had left because he wasn't being challenged, each job paid more or provided a new learning experience that was superior to the last job, I would have welcomed such an individual.

- Talk about your accomplishments.
- Tell what you liked about your current and past jobs.
- Tell where you see your industry going.
- Ask informed questions about the company.
- Ask what is expected of you.
- If you talk about mistakes you have made, mention what you have learned.

Avoid saying the following:

- Don't complain about your old company or boss.
- Don't dwell on things that didn't go well.
- Don't lie about anything on your resume.
- Don't talk about things you know very little about.
- Don't talk about politics or religion.
- Don't brag about your accomplishments.

A lot of people shoot themselves in the foot during an interview by talking negatively about their old company or boss. Sometimes these statements are made unsolicited, but often they are made after an interviewer asks them why they left their last company. When asked this question, give careful thought to your answer and don't say anything that could be construed as negative about your old boss and company.

3

Networking to Increase Sales

Companies don't expect salespeople who have recently graduated from college to bring a Rolodex of contacts that will lead to sales, but if you have been out in the workforce for more than five years, you'd better have a good one. The two most important criteria for evaluating salespeople are contacts and product knowledge.

Small companies can't afford to hire salespeople who can't pay for themselves over the course of six months to a year. Even companies willing to wait that long for a payback are considered generous. Companies want employees who have an up-to-date, quality contact database.

Five Keys to Successful Sales Networking

There are five keys to being a successful networker for sales. You don't need to have all five to be a success, but mastering at least two is critical. The five keys are knowledge, personality, physical appearance, appropriate attire, and manners.

Knowledge

Sales knowledge goes beyond knowing about one's business. It means being well read and informed—having interest in things other than your business. In a room of 100 people, I am sure 50 to 70 percent have as much or more brain power than I do, but I enjoy sports, reading, theater, traveling, my children, and many other interests outside of work. The following is an example of how knowledge has helped me.

One day I went to call on a marketing director from a big service firm to ask him if his firm wanted to be a sponsor. You couldn't help but notice that his office was a shrine to Mickey Mantle, the recently deceased baseball player. He even had a life-size cardboard cutout of the former Yankee slugger. Being a former sportswriter and avid reader of many sports books and publications, I was able to have an enlivened and in-depth conversation with him about Mickey Mantle, who also happened to be my favorite player. By the time we were done, the marketing director was willing to help a fellow Mickey Mantle fan's organization with financial support.

Physical Appearance

Your physical appearance tells people a lot about you. People prefer to associate with people they think are attractive or at least nonoffensive. Make sure your clothes enhance your appearance. Take time to exercise; you will feel better about yourself and, if you feel good about you, so will others. People who aren't comfortable with their appearance have a hard time hiding their feelings, and that is usually apparent to people they meet. If you improve your level of fitness and learn to be comfortable with yourself, the way you move and speak can portray that you are healthy and energetic, even if you are overweight or have a physical disability.

I once had a secretary who could do the work of five people. To this day, I have never seen anyone better. Unfortunately, she had a weight problem and every time she interviewed with a company for a more responsible job, she told me, she never made it to the second interview. I believe that her medical and physical conditioning was a factor. Unfortunately, the people who didn't hire her won't know what a terrific asset she could have been to their company.

Appropriate Attire

Make sure you are dressed appropriately for the given business situation. If you are going to an event at a business club, make sure you are wearing a nice suit and tie. Women should wear a knee-length (or longer) dress or business suit when

I once made the mistake of not being aware of current business dress trends. When I first became manager of the Penn State Technology Development Center, I had lunch with one of the top partners at a Big Six consulting firm to pitch him on being a financial sponsor of the Center. He took me to one of the finest private clubs in Philadelphia. This was my first big lunch meeting and I wore my best suit, which had a vest and tie. Unfortunately, coming from a small town, I was a little behind in what was in fashion. When we went to the club I realized I was the only person wearing a vest—and my tie was as wide as my napkin! I felt embarrassed and couldn't concentrate on the meeting. My first stop after the meeting was the men's clothing store!

attending non-black-tie functions. Don't overdress for events that don't require it, however, because people you meet with may feel uncomfortable with you.

Personality

Ultimately, personality is the most important key to success in sales and in life. Looking good and dressing well might get you in the door, but you'd better be substantive once you get in. How many times have you met someone you thought wasn't particularly attractive, but because of his or her personality you enjoyed being around the person? People enjoy those who don't take themselves too seriously, have a good sense of humor, and are fun to be around.

For example, take the most recent presidential elections. Bob Dole, the Senate majority leader, one of the nation's legislative leaders for the better part of 30 years, was easily defeated by President Bill Clinton. Senator Dole was in office when President Clinton was still in high school, and ran for vice president the first time when President Clinton was in college. Maybe the largest contributing factor to Senator Dole losing was that people couldn't warm up to him. He didn't make people feel comfortable. The president has charm and personality. Even if you don't agree with him, you can at least like him on a personal level, which helps him sell his message.

Manners

This is an area for which I have personally sought out professional coaching, and I recommend it to others. When you see a person with good manners you usually associate that with good breeding and the word "class." Interrupting people,

During my time as executive director of the Eastern Technology Council, we created a program series called "Titans of Technology." The series featured presidents of prominent technology companies. One of our first speakers was Ronald Skates, chairman/CEO of Data General, a computer company. Every speaker received a gift as a thank-you for speaking. Mr. Skates sent a thank-you note for inviting him to speak and for the gift. He didn't have to do it, because we were thanking him, but he did it anyway. It left a great impression on me and my staff. It was a gesture that we still talk about today.

speaking with your mouth full of food, and using your fingers to block food onto your fork are very unbecoming.

Developing contacts and keeping up with those contacts is very critical for professional success. The rest of this chapter provides suggestions on how to develop that network and keep it alive. Each section of this chapter will have advice for both recent college graduates and seasoned working professionals.

Who to Contact

When you are just out of college, your base of contacts is small, but it probably isn't as small as you think. Most people's first job requires contacting a lot of strangers and asking them if they will take the time to see you. In most cases people will say no because they prefer a proper introduction or they are just too busy.

Recent college graduates should make a list of everyone they know and who those people might know. The following is a list of people to contact to develop a sales list.

- *Your parents' business contacts.* Many times your parents' business contacts may be appropriate people to call.
- *Your parents' friends.* Growing up, you might not have been interested in what your parents' friends do for a living, yet they can be a terrific source of contacts.
- *Your friend's parents.* Like your parents' friends you probably never knew what your friends' parents did, but now it's time to find out.
- *College friends.* Many of your college friends will be hired by companies who may be able to use your products and services. Keep in contact with them.
- *Country and swim clubs.* If you belong to a country or swim club, you probably meet a lot of people who work for companies that would be interested in your services. Reacquaint yourself. If you aren't a member of a club, join one. YMCAs are usually a terrific place to start.
- *Your place of worship.* Many serious professionals are heavily involved in their places of worship.
- *Former employers.* Most of us have had part-time jobs, and our former employers are occasionally good references for new business.
- *Sports leagues.* Aggressive executives and salespeople usually like to participate in some type of sport—mostly golf, tennis, and softball. Getting involved in sports can yield good contacts.
- *Junior Chamber of Commerce.* This is a great organization to join after college. It's for businesspeople under the age of 40.

The above suggestions are a start to developing a base of contacts. Once you are a working professional, you need to add to the above relationships. If you are a seasoned business professional, the following will help you build a base of clients that you can bring from company to company.

- *Clients.* Happy current clients are the best source of references and leads for future clients.
- *Past clients.* Keep in touch with past clients and let them know where you are and what you are doing. If you have done a good job, they will be glad to make a referral.
- *Trade associations.* Join trade associations related to your industry and organizations whose members might be interested in your product.
- *Nonprofit organizations.* I mentioned this already, but it's worth mentioning again. It's good for society for people to get involved, and if you need to account for your time to your employer, the contacts are usually there to bring in additional business.
- *Chambers of commerce.* I mentioned this previously, but one group that can provide quality contacts and is usually overlooked are service providers—accountants, lawyers, and bankers. Service providers have good contacts that can lead to sales.

What to Say to Build Your Sales Network

There are lots of things to say when meeting someone for the first time that will make a good first impression. Following are topics of conversation people usually feel comfortable with at different types of events:

Business Event. If you initiate a conversation at a business event, always ask the person what his or her company does and what he or she does for the company. People are most comfortable discussing things they know.

Business Social Event. You can start a conversation at a business event by asking if this is the first time the person has attended such an event and what drew him or her to the event. At a business social event, you need to be subtle regarding your business interest because many people come to business social events for the social value, not just the business contacts. Once you have developed a rapport, then lead into asking what company the person represents and what he or she does for the company.

Social Event. During your career you will be invited to well-attended social events. For instance, one of my favorite events is the Philadelphia Public Libraries Borrowers Ball. The purpose of the ball is to raise money for buying books and equipment for the library. I make sure I bring my business cards, because many of the attendees are leaders of the business community. If I know someone, I'll start the conversation by asking how his or her business is doing and then suggesting we get together for breakfast or lunch. If I don't know someone I'll start by asking about his or her company and position.

What to Avoid Discussing

When meeting someone for the first time you should stay away from the following topics:

Politics and Religion. My grandfather once told me to stay away from conversations about politics and religion with strangers. I believe that will always hold true. People may have strong feelings in these areas, and you may make comments that the person feels are inappropriate and hence could cripple a potentially good relationship.

Yourself. Don't talk only about yourself or your product. Many people are so anxious to sell themselves and their products that they end up talking at, not to, the person they are meeting.

Negative Comments About Other People. During an initial meeting I had with a company president, he made his negative feelings known about a president of another company that I knew personally. I considered it very unprofessional and couldn't wait to get out of this person's office. Most people are uncomfortable when hearing negative comments about other people from someone they just met.

Praising Other People. Early in my career, I was meeting with the president of a large insurance company. During the course of the conversation, which was going well, I accidentally mentioned another insurance company and that I liked the president of that company. Many times that won't get you in any trouble because competitors are usually friendly when they see each other. What I didn't know was that these two executives were sworn enemies, who would do anything to ruin each other. The best thing to do is keep the conversation focused on the purpose of your meeting. You will get in a lot less trouble.

Going the Extra Mile

Competition has become so intense that there isn't a great deal of difference between products or services from one vendor to the next. If you go to a top-tier law firm, for example, the attorneys' skills are probably no better than those of their competition. Therefore, it is important to give yourself an edge over the competition. Going the extra mile doesn't always get you the business, but it does enhance your chances. There are four things I try to do consistently. I keep up with my customers' hobbies and sports interests, and I occasionally send them small presents or articles of interest.

Hobbies. Try to find out what hobbies the target customer enjoys. For example, I once learned that the CEO of a major pharmaceutical company enjoyed gardening. I went to the local bookstore's table of books under $5 and found a book on gardening, and sent the CEO the book with information about our company. He sent a thank-you and asked one of his executives to take the time to visit with me.

Sports. (I differentiate sports from hobbies because I look at hobbies as something you do for and by yourself and sports as something that is interactive and involves others to make it interesting and enjoyable.) Many people have a favorite college or pro team. For two years, I tried to get in front of a certain CEO, who headed a $500 million family-owned business. I went to every event he was either honored at or was chairman of. I managed to get his business card and gave him mine and still no luck. One day I read a story in the newspaper about him and it mentioned what a great fan he was of his college's basketball team.

Being a sports fan myself, I remembered a book written about his college team going to the NCAA Finals. I bought the book and sent it to him and told him a true short story about how I knew one of the players on the team. He sent me a note and invited me to lunch.

Small Presents. When I ran the Penn State Technology Development Center and the Eastern Technology Council I had bibs for babies printed up with the organization's name on them. Every time a member or prospective member had a baby, I sent one. That built up a lot of goodwill. Over the years, people have come up to me and reminded me about the bib we sent them.

I also gave dinner gift certificates for two if someone was very helpful in assisting my organization in landing a client, bringing in a major sponsor, or helping make an event better. Some gifts are quickly forgotten, but an evening at a fine restaurant is always remembered.

Articles of Interest. One way to stay in front of your customer or potential customer and develop a relationship is to send published articles that mention the person or his or her company. You can also send articles about the industry or a specific competitor. This shows you are aware of the person's business. All customers like to know that you are thinking about them.

Appropriate Information to Provide

Many people believe the heavier the packet of information, the more impressed a potential client will be. I am not one of those people. Give people only the most important information. Just think how busy you are and what information most likely gets your attention.

Whenever I provide people with marketing information on my company, I send a three-paragraph letter that contains an example of how my product or service can help them and mention what information they should look at in the package I sent them. Letters 3.1 and 3.2 are samples of such cover letters.

INFORMATION COVER LETTER

Jane Smith
Chairman/CEO
Smith Industries
45 Smith Drive
Smithville, PA 19555

Dear Jane:

I hope all is well. The reason I am writing to you is that I noticed your company doesn't have a presence on the Internet. I think a company like Smith, which has a wide range of consumer products, should have a site that displays the products that sell the most and have the highest profit margin. Your portable ice maker is a super product that I believe people from around the world would love to buy.

Enclosed is information on our company, which is one of the leading outsourcing Internet development firms on the east coast. When looking at our information, please make a note of the URLs for the websites we have developed and take a look at the recommendation letters in the right pocket of the folder.

I will call your office to set up an appointment to discuss some of our ideas with you or whomever you feel is appropriate. Our goal is to help you use the Web as a tool to make money, not just inform potential customers of your existence. If you have a question, please don't hesitate to call me at 610-555-5555 (ext. 200).

Sincerely,

Marc Kramer
President

INFORMATION COVER LETTER

John Smith
Chairman/CEO
Smith Industries
45 Smith Drive
Smithville, PA 19555

Dear John:

The reason I am writing to you is that I noticed your company doesn't have a presence on the Internet. I think a company like Smith, which has a wide range of consumer products, should have a site that displays the products that sell the most and have the highest profit margin. Your portable ice maker is a super product that I believe people from around the world would love to buy.

Enclosed is our brochure. Please take time to look at the following:

- Color copies of the home pages we have developed.
- Client list.
- Reference letters.

If you'd like, we can catalog products and maintain the site, so you don't have to worry about it. I will give you a call in the next few days. If you have a question, please don't hesitate to call me at 610-555-5555 (ext. 200).

Sincerely,

Marc Kramer
President

4

Networking to Raise Money

A lot of books have been written on how to raise money. One book that I think is particularly good is *Finding Money* by Kate Lister and Tom Harnish. This book offers tips from people who provide funding and who have gotten funding.

Raising money is not easy, regardless of how good your product or service. Service companies have a harder time raising money than product companies, because the barrier to entry in a service company is considered to be low. The reason it is considered low is because it can be easily duplicated, whereas a design for a computer chip, for example, can't be, and chip designs are protected by patents. People like to invest in product companies because they can touch the product and if the company doesn't do well, the product can be licensed or sold to another company.

Writing a cogent business plan and having a quality management group is essential to successfully raising money. Just as important as the plan and management is the ability to get access to the right people to raise money.

I have raised money to launch publications, events, trade associations, multimedia companies, and business incubators. The ability to raise money rests more with who you know than the quality of your product/service or management team. Most money you can raise to start a venture comes from individuals and venture capital funds.

People who have money to invest either for themselves or in proxy for other investors usually trust people they know. Would you give money to a stranger? Not likely. The same holds true for investors. For the most part investors want equity in a company. Some are willing to make loans, but usually those loans have the option to convert into equity.

Who to Contact

Where do you meet investors? There are many types of potential investors. The following sections describe ten sources who either have money or access to money, where to meet them, and what they typically like to invest in.

Private Investors

Private investors are wealthy individuals, also known as accredited investors. These people, who have a net worth of at least $1 million and/or have disposable income of at least $250,000 a year, are usually businesspeople and occasionally professionals such as doctors and lawyers. Private investors usually like to invest in businesses related to the field they've been successful in. They typically invest $25,000–$250,000 and look for at least five times' return on their money.

Private investors can be found in a variety of places:

- Country clubs
- Leadership positions in nonprofit associations and cultural institutions
- Business book lists
- On the boards of places of worship
- On the boards of schools of higher education

Corporate Venture Capital

Many Fortune 500 companies have venture capital groups that invest in companies that would have a strategic interest for the companies they represent. Corporate venture capitalists invest in businesses related to their core business or companies that use their technologies to create a new line of business. Their investments are both cash and resources and are usually from $500,000 to millions of dollars. A friend of mine received a $40 million investment from a Japanese company because it felt his technology fit well within its business.

Corporate venture capitalists can be found in the following places:

- National and regional venture capital conferences
- American Licensing Society events
- Regional venture capital functions such as lunches and seminars
- Regional technology council and major national trade association events

Traditional Venture Capital

Traditional sources of venture capital include individual, corporate, and private and nonprofit government and pension money. Venture capitalists are entrusted with investing the money given to them by their limited partners. Venture funds usually have certain investment criteria that pertain to size of investment, industry, and geographic location of the company they invest in. Venture capitalists can be found in the same places as corporate venture capitalists.

Traditional venture capitalists are divided into two groups. The first group invests in early-stage companies that have little or no sales, with the average investment between $500,000 and $1 million. The second group invests in later-stage companies, which are less risky because they have proven sales and a seasoned management team. Later stage venture capitalists invest $1–$5 million on average.

State Venture Funds

Many states, and even counties and cities, in the United States have created venture funds that make equity investments or loan entrepreneurs money. You can find these nonprofit venture funds through your local chamber of commerce or city, county, or state commerce department.

Unlike corporate and traditional venture capitalists, who usually won't meet with entrepreneurs unless they have been introduced by someone they know and trust, these venture capitalists are public or semipublic servants and it's their job to meet with entrepreneurs. Although they are in the public sector, they too are influenced by people they know and respect. State venture funds usually invest only $25,000–$250,000.

Banks

When most people think of banks, they think of loans, which require assets of some type as collateral. Many banks also have venture capital arms that make investments. These venture capitalists can be contacted directly, or you can meet them at all of the forums we have mentioned for other venture funds. If you are a bank customer, it is easy to get in front of these people.

Business Consultants

There are business consultants that assist entrepreneurs in writing business plans, but more importantly, in raising money. These people are usually experienced business executives who have come out of the banking, big company corporate strategic planning, and venture capital fields. Business consultants who focus on raising money for entrepreneurial companies can be found in the following places:

- Local venture capital association meetings
- Country clubs
- Through county economic development authorities
- University business school seminars

Venture Leasing

Venture leasing companies can provide equipment in exchange for equity and/or warrants in a business. You can find these professionals at the same functions as traditional venture capitalists.

Corporate Attorneys

Corporate attorneys don't usually invest themselves, but they usually have clients who are interested in investing. Corporate attorneys from large law firms typically have an abundance of good contacts in the venture, corporate, and private investor community. The best places to meet these people are:

- Local venture capital association meetings
- Small business development corporation seminars
- Through university business school faculty and seminars
- Trade association meetings
- Events put on by their law firms

Accountants

Accountants and attorneys work closely together and have many of the same contacts. Their recommendation to an investor to read your plan will carry a lot of weight for two reasons: They have existing relationships with venture capitalists because of past deals done together, and they have agreed to recommend or take you on as a client. This is very important because venture capitalists receive thousands of unsolicited plans each year, and if they receive a plan from someone they trust, they are more apt to review it.

Small Business Development Corporations

Small business development corporations (SBDCs) are in most states with a large corporate population. Their mission is to help entrepreneurs succeed by providing assistance in writing business plans, meeting investors, and organizing the business. These corporations can be found by contacting your county industrial development authority, local bank, regional venture capital association, local business incubator, or your state's department of commerce.

What to Say When Meeting Potential Investors

When meeting prospective investors, it is a good idea to ascertain early whether they invest in early- or later-stage companies, what industries they are interested in, and what amounts of money they are willing to invest. You can then determine whether to tell the person about your company. If your venture doesn't fit the investor's profile, you should ask if he or she knows of others who would be interested in speaking with you.

Make sure your conversation is short and to the point, and that a 13-year-old could explain what you do. If your explanation is too complex and convoluted, you'll risk losing the prospective investor's interest. Here are some simple examples of how to explain who you are and what your company does.

Example 1

> "My name is John Smith and I am president of Easy-Database. We are developing software that helps non-technical people find information in complex databases. The market for our product is companies with 50 or more people that sell at least ten different products."

Example 2

> "My name is Jane Smith and I am president of Business Planners. My company has developed software that assists entrepreneurs in writing easily understood business plans."

The two examples above are easy enough to follow that a prospect can ask intelligent follow-up questions or have enough of an understanding to relate it to another person. I can't tell you how many times people have given me such complex answers to the question of what their company does that I walk away wondering what they do. Often people try to impress others by making their business sound more complex than it needs to be. People like to invest in businesses that are easily explained to the general public. Here are examples of what *not* to say using the examples previously mentioned.

Example 1 (Wrong)

> "Hi! My name is John Smith and I am president of Easy-Database. We are developing a highly structured product that overlaps different types of databases such as data marts and warehouses to unearth mission critical information."

For people who are in MIS or corporate strategic planning that explanation may be easy to understand, but others will have no idea what the speaker means. You have to go under the assumption the person you are meeting for the first time doesn't know anything about your field.

Example 2 (Wrong)

> "Good morning! My name is Jane Smith and I am president of Integrated Information Resources. Our product is used by researchers who use various types of databases and can't find information."

This seems relatively simple and may possibly invite questions regarding what the product actually does. Here is a better example of what Jane could have said.

Example 3 (Right)

> "Good morning! My name is Jane Smith and I am president of Integrated Information Resources. We have developed software tools that allow researchers full information from structured and unstructured databases, which shortens the time it takes to do research

and eventually create products. It's a great time and money saver."

What to Do After Your Initial Meeting with Potential Investors

Request a business card from the potential investor and ask if he or she would be interested in reading either your entire business plan or just the executive summary.

If the person has an e-mail address, you should consider sending the information electronically. I find e-mail is the best form of communication. People tend to read all of their e-mails and they become less distracted because they are focused on whatever is on the screen. Also, e-mail makes it easy for the recipient of your information to respond quickly. He or she doesn't have to print out a letter, address an envelope, put on a stamp, and mail it, but can respond almost instantly with the touch of a few keys. Letter 4.1 is an example of a good follow-up letter or e-mail.

If the potential investor wants only an executive summary, you should either e-mail it or fax it. Faxing, in my opinion, is the next best way of sending information. Regular mail usually gets opened last or is put aside until later in the week. You can send summaries and plans by express mail, but that is costly and if the person has a secretary it may not have any greater impact than regular mail.

Appropriate Information to Provide

There are a lot of good books on how to write a business plan. Your local library or retail bookstore should have a number of

Letter 4.1

INVESTOR FOLLOW-UP LETTER

Dear John:

It was a pleasure meeting you at the venture forum. I appreciate your willingness to take a look at my business plan.

To refresh your memory, my company has developed a software product that assists entrepreneurs in writing good business plans. Enclosed [or in the case of e-mail, attached] is my business plan. I will call you in the next few days to see if you would be interested in meeting. Please don't hesitate to call me at 610-555-5555.

Sincerely,

Jane Smith
President

them from major business publishers, including NTC Business Books. Every business plan should contain the following sections and should be no more than 15 to 20 pages.

- Executive summary
- Description of product or service
- Market description
- Sales and marketing strategy
- Competition
- Management team
- Uses of raised capital
- Financials

The plan's appearance should be neat and professional looking, but it doesn't have to be bound or have a cover. A stapled business plan that comes out of a typical computer printer is sufficient.

5

Writing Good Introductory and Follow-Up Letters

The art of letter writing was on the decline for many years because of telephone use and the low cost of traveling by airplane. Over the years, how many times have you written to your friends? It's easier just to call them.

With the popularity of the Internet and its electronic mail component, however, good writing skills are again a necessity. People are now being judged on something other than physical appearance and speaking skills. If your correspondence is poorly written, your ability to secure the position you are looking for or the sale you expected will be greatly diminished.

Because many people don't write much on a daily basis, our written communication skills may not be what they should be. We may struggle just trying to write a few short, simple letters. I recommend two things to improve your writing skills: take a writing course at a local college, and buy a computer and correspond with friends and business associates through the Internet.

Keys to Writing a Good Letter

The keys to writing a letter that produces a positive response include opening the letter by telling who you are and who, if anyone, referred you, or how you knew to write to this person. The second paragraph should discuss in concise form what your product or service can do for the reader to help them make or save money, or both. For example, my former company, Mixed Media Works, designed websites for companies. It could show a travel agency that the Web had the ability to increase its sales by 10 percent, decrease overhead by 20 percent, and cut customer cost by 15 percent—compelling arguments for meeting with my company.

Here are some tips to remember:

- Always make sure you have spelled the name of the person you are writing to correctly. If you have any doubts, call his or her office to confirm the spelling.
- Always check your spelling and grammar. When people see misspellings and poor grammar, they assume you don't pay attention to detail. People worry how you will represent them to clients and how you will handle their business.
- Personalize your letters. Experienced professionals know form letters when they see them.
- Never ask the person you are writing to contact you. Why should someone you are trying to get to offer you a position or buy your product or service call you? You would be surprised how many letters I have received over the years from people asking me to call them when they wanted something from me.
- Always thank the person for taking the time to read your letter.

Lastly, if you have someone who can proof your correspondence before it goes out, take advantage of it. All too often, we are so consumed in what we are writing that we aren't reading the words and sentences as they actually appear.

Letters to Potential Employers

When writing a good introductory letter, you need to find common ground with the reader to develop rapport. For example, I found out before a job interview that the person I was meeting with was a big John Wayne fan. I mentioned this in my letter and that I would be bringing a copy of a book I had just read on John Wayne. This worked out quite well. The interviewer believed that people who liked John Wayne probably held the same values as the actor, which would translate into their work.

Writing a Good Introductory Letter

Good introductory letters should be no more than a page, single-spaced, and usually only three or four paragraphs. Remember, most people are very busy with their work and home lives, so be short and to the point. Following are sample introductory job search letters.

Letters 5.1 and 5.2 show examples of introductory letters for new graduates. In Letter 5.1 the writer doesn't waste the reader's time about what he wants. The higher the executive, the more important it is to get directly to the point. This allows the reader to know exactly what you are looking for and how, if at all, you can help him or her. If the employer immediately sees no fit, he or she can respond accordingly. Ambiguous letters waste everyone's time.

The difference between Letters 5.1 and 5.2 is that the second one makes it clear the writer is focused on getting a position in the aerospace industry. (The writer of 5.1 is just interested in obtaining a position.) The writer of 5.2 also establishes that he has taken the time to become familiar with the industry through research for a class project. He has a better chance of getting an interview than the writer of Letter 5.1 because he let the reader know he is knowledgeable about the aerospace industry.

JOB SEARCH LETTER FOR
RECENT COLLEGE GRADUATE

John Smith
President
Smith Industries
5 Smith Place
Smithville, PA 19555

Dear Mr. Smith:

I have just graduated from Penn State University with a degree in journalism and I am interested in a public relations and/or marketing position with your company. I am aware of your company's fine reputation in the airplane parts industry and I have always had an interest in aviation.

Enclosed is my resume. I will call your office within five business days to see who I might speak to about interviewing for a position with your company. Thank you for taking the time to read my letter.

Sincerely,

Marc Kramer

Job Search Letter for
Recent College Graduate

John Smith
President
Smith Industries
5 Smith Place
Smithville, PA 19555

Dear Mr. Smith:

I am very interested in getting into the aerospace industry and I would like to apply for a position in your sales department. I recently graduated from West Virginia University with a degree in business. My senior marketing paper, which is enclosed, was on the state of the aerospace industry in America.

I am a very hard worker and made my own money in college by selling t-shirts at sporting events. Enclosed is my resume. I will call your office to see who in your organization I should speak with concerning a possible interview with your company. Thank you for taking the time to read my letter. I hope I get a chance to meet you in person.

Sincerely,

Marc Kramer

Working professionals will write a different letter than a recent college graduate. If you are an experienced professional, you should highlight your relevant accomplishments. If you are in sales your prospective employer will want to know some of your industry contacts that can bring in immediate sales or, if you are outside the industry, what skills you bring that will enhance sales. If you are not in sales, then mentioning papers you have written for trade journals, advanced degrees, and other experience that qualifies you for the job you seek can be helpful. Letters 5.3 and 5.4 show examples of introductory letters for working professionals with and without referrals. The writer of Letter 5.3 immediately shows his track record in the field and his potential to bring in sales through his network. The reader will likely call the writer as soon as possible.

In Letter 5.4 the writer immediately mentions a name the reader should be familiar with, gets down to business concerning the purpose of the letter, and documents his success in his current position. The writer also lets the reader know why he is leaving, which is one of the first questions every future employer wants to know.

Thank-You Letters

After meeting with a potential employer, you need to send him or her a thank-you note, whether by regular mail, e-mail, or fax. Over the years I have been surprised by the number of job candidates who forget to thank me for the opportunity to interview with my company. It isn't me who is looking for new employment, it's them. There have been people I have interviewed that I thought would be good for my organization and, because they didn't send a thank-you letter, I dropped them from my candidates list. Sending a thank-you note is both

JOB SEARCH LETTER FOR WORKING PROFESSIONAL WITHOUT REFERRAL

John Smith
President
Smith Industries
5 Smith Place
Smithville, PA 19555

Dear Mr. Smith:

I am looking for a new opportunity and challenge in the computer software sales field. Over the last three years I have sold $3 million of software to such companies as General Motors, Boeing, and Merck & Co. I am very impressed with Smith Industries' new satellite tracking software and I know with my experience and current book of business I can bring in a lot of sales.

I will telephone your office to make sure you receive this letter and to see who I should meet with in your organization. Thank you for taking time to read this letter. I hope we have an opportunity to meet.

Sincerely,

Marc Kramer

Job Search Letter for Working Professional with Referral

John Smith
President
Smith Industries
5 Smith Place
Smithville, PA 19555

Dear Mr. Smith:

Last night I saw Ray Jones, president of Jones Inc., at a chamber of commerce dinner and he told me you are looking for a manager for your computer department. He suggested I write to you and send you my resume.

I have experience in three different platforms and the department I manage oversees 100 different desktop and laptop computers. Our efficiency rating has grown from 73 to 92 percent in the five years I have managed the department. I'm looking for new challenges and professional growth opportunities that my current company and position do not offer.

Enclosed is my resume. I will call your office to see if you are interested in meeting.

Sincerely,

Marc Kramer

expected and a good way for you to stay in front of your prospective employer.

Some people feel sending a handwritten thank-you is better than a typed one. It's fine to send a handwritten thank-you for tickets to a hockey game or being invited to a professional associate's home for dinner, but typed thank-you notes are more appropriate for job interviews and sales meetings. Letters 5.5 and 5.6 are examples of good thank-you letters.

Letter 5.5 is a simple thank-you that lets the recipient know you appreciate his time, would like to work for his company, and will be aggressive in following up on potential opportunities at his company. Letter 5.6 is similar to 5.5, but also stresses the immediate value of your contacts and experience. Most employers prefer to hire someone who can make an immediate impact on their company.

If you want to set yourself apart from other candidates, here are a few suggestions.

- After meeting the interviewer, send a copy of a story you read about the industry or a major competitor along with your thank-you.
- Once you send your thank-you and follow up with a telephone call for a second meeting, send the interviewer stories on the competition or the industry regardless of whether he or she returns your call. This will show the interviewer you are thinking about the company and are aware of the problems and major issues of the industry.
- Make a one-page list of ideas that can save or make the company money. The last three positions I interviewed for, I wrote down my ideas and how I would implement them. All three companies offered me jobs. It doesn't matter if your future employer agrees with your ideas. What

JOB INTERVIEW THANK-YOU LETTER FROM RECENT COLLEGE GRADUATE

John Smith
President
Smith Industries
5 Smith Place
Smithville, PA 19555

Dear Mr. Smith:

Thank you for taking the time to interview me. I enjoyed getting a chance to meet you and find out more about Smith Industries. Although I have only recently graduated from college, I bring with me a high degree of energy and a lifetime interest in your industry. Companies like Smith are accustomed to long-term investments in their projects; I hope you have the same attitude toward people.

Again, thank you for your consideration. I look forward to hearing from you.

Sincerely,

Marc Kramer

JOB INTERVIEW THANK-YOU LETTER FROM AN EXPERIENCED PROFESSIONAL

John Smith
President
Smith Industries
5 Smith Place
Smithville, PA 19555

Dear Mr. Smith:

Thank you for taking the time to interview me. I enjoyed getting a chance to meet you and find out more about Smith Industries. I am very excited about the opportunities offered at Smith Industries. I will bring with me 10 years' experience in the aerospace industry, more than 25 high-level industry contacts, and a proven track record in sales.

I believe with my industry contacts and experience, I would make a positive addition to both the company and the bottom line. If you need additional references from me, please let me know.

Again, thank you for taking the time to meet with me.

Sincerely,

Marc Kramer

matters is that you showed that you thought about the company and have ideas.

- Future employers and customers always appreciate someone who spends time understanding their business. The term "internalizing" is the buzz word for this.

Letters for Prospective Clients

The next group of sample letters are examples of ones you would use when contacting a prospective client. In most cases it's a waste of time writing to someone if you don't have something in common with him or her, such as:

- having attended the same college
- a mutual friend or business associate
- belonging to the same country club and/or business organization

The only time a cold call is really effective is if you are offering a service or product that is unique to the marketplace and you don't have any competitors.

Letter 5.7 starts by mentioning a mutual business associate. Mutual business associates, especially ones who are presidents of their own companies, carry a lot of weight with people. Once you mention who sent you, explain why you are writing.

Letter 5.8 starts by mentioning the recipient's alma mater. Unless the person had a dreadful college experience, this is a very good way to get someone's attention and set yourself up for a possible sale. People always like to help others who they have something in common with, such as attending the same high school, church, or country club. As in Letter 5.7, it is important to follow that connection with your reason for writing.

The letters that get responses are ones that bring the writer and recipient together and tell why they should do business together. Once you have found a job opportunity, you should let your contacts know where you have landed and thank them for assisting you in your search. Don't forget to let them know what you and your new employer do. The people you are thanking may be potential customers. It's important to keep in contact with potential clients regardless of whether a sale is made. You never know when someone will buy, or when they might refer a customer to you.

Letter 5.7

John Smith
President
Smith Industries
5 Smith Place
Smithville, PA 19555

Dear Mr. Smith:

John Jones, president of Jones Worldwide, is one of my clients. He suggested I contact you because you would be interested in our service. My company designs, develops, and maintains websites for the Internet.

Our clients are companies that I am sure you are familiar with, such as IBM, General Motors, and Citicorp. I would be interested in speaking with the appropriate person in your organization to discuss how we can help implement your Internet strategy.

I will call your office in the next five days to find out who we should meet with. Thank you for taking the time to read this letter.

Sincerely,

Marc Kramer
Account Executive

John Smith
President
Smith Industries
5 Smith Place
Smithville, PA 19555

Dear Mr. Smith:

I read in the newspaper that you are a graduate of West Virginia University. I am as well and I am hoping I can ask a follow Mountaineer for a favor. My company creates, implements, and manages Internet sites for companies like yours.

I noticed you don't have a website. Could you please pass my letter and the enclosed packet about my company to the appropriate person in your organization? We handle Fortune 1000 companies such as Ford, Digital Computer, and Microsoft. I will call your office in the next week to find out to whom you forwarded my letter.

Thanks for taking the time to read this letter. If you are interested in seeing the Mountaineers play Temple in football, I have extra tickets and I would be glad to have you as my guest.

Sincerely,

Marc Kramer
Account Executive

6

Maintaining Networking Relationships

Aside from knowledge in your profession, your wealth is in your network. There are few professions—medical doctors, money managers, and computer programmers—where ability is more important than personal relationships. Long-lasting business relationships constantly need nurturing through telephone calls, letters, e-mail, and meeting at events. If you stop communicating, the sense of intimacy and familiarity gets lost and relationships fade, which can lock you out of good opportunities. This chapter gives examples of how to cultivate and maintain network relationships.

There are three main types of relationships in business that you need to think about how to maintain:

Employer/Employee Relationships

You can be on either or both sides of the employer/employee paradigm. It's important to develop a good relationship with your boss to advance your career, and it's equally important to develop a good relationship with your employees so you can maximize their abilities.

Client Relationships

We all make our livings from our clients. Business is becoming more competitive because distance is becoming irrelevant due to the Internet, inexpensive business travel, and video conferencing. Therefore, it's important to constantly stay in front of your clients and to have their goodwill.

Vendor Relationships

Many people look at their vendors as just more people who are taking money out of their pockets. Many people don't treat their vendors with respect and, in fact, think of the relationship as adversarial. That kind of thinking is a huge mistake.

Vendors can be great allies in referring business because if your business grows, they will in turn make more money. And when times are tough and you can't pay your bills on time, a good relationship with your vendors will help you get what you need to operate your business and avoid unnecessary lawsuits.

Once you have developed a good relationship with someone, it's important to maintain it. Maintaining relationships is crucial to long-term success, and it takes time and careful thought.

Maintain Integrity

You want to appear sincere in your actions. If you are just building a relationship with someone because you want their business, you want to move up in the corporation, or just want to get the most out of someone, your motives will be apparent to the person you are dealing with.

When I ran the Eastern Technology Council, which, at the time, was the second largest technology council in the world, I saw how clients, vendors, employers and employees all tried to get the most out of my position. With most of those people, I knew they weren't interested in getting to know Marc Kramer. They were interested in making sure the Executive Director of the Eastern Technology Council got to know them so they would receive recommendations for new business or to open doors.

There is nothing wrong with this because that is what I was being paid for, but some people made a point of telling me they were interested in meeting me because they heard good things about me. However, once I left my position these people were impossible to get in contact with.

Members and vendors of the Council wanted me to remember them when it came time to referring business, so they sent me gifts at Christmas, took me to ball games, and offered me tickets to a variety of events. For the most part I accepted these gifts as perks of the position and a chance to develop a reciprocal relationship. What I appreciated most was when they told me up front the reason for inviting me to an event was to get to know me better so we might do business.

Business people, by and large, accept and understand if your motives for being helpful are purely to get business. The fact is most of the people you do business with are people you never knew before. They have no personal connection with you.

There are different ways of maintaining relationships that allow you to maintain your integrity with the person you are dealing with. You have to be careful not to overstep the bounds between client/vendor or employer/employee relationship and personal friend. Once you become a personal friend, everyone expects more from the relationship. It's best to make sure people aren't misled.

I have never invited someone to my home or to go out socially unless I wanted to get to know him or her on a personal level. Once I make such an invitation, I personally feel a responsibility to be more than a business associate. Therefore, my suggestions in the remainder of this chapter are based on the understanding that the business relationships you will develop are just that—business relationships.

Give Appropriate Gifts

There is nothing wrong with giving gifts to thank someone for doing you a special favor or to get someone's attention. The question arises regarding when you should send a gift and who should receive one. I believe you can send gifts to both customers and vendors. If you are getting great service from a vendor, why not show them additional appreciation? You want to let clients know you appreciate them.

Before sending a gift, check with someone in your business associate's organization to make sure the company doesn't have a policy against accepting gifts and to see what types of gifts are acceptable. For example, newspaper reporters are not allowed to accept gifts of any type for fear of corrupting their integrity. Gifts should be sent in the following circumstances:

- To capture the attention of a major potential client when your letters, faxes, and e-mails have gone unanswered. I once sent a book to a hard-to-reach potential customer and finally received a response—the person sent me a thank-you *and* the name of the person in their organization to contact.
- A business associate opens a door leading to a sale.
- A business associate becomes a parent; his or her child is confirmed, has a Bar Mitzvah, or gets married.
- A business associate celebrates a five-, ten-, fifteen-, or twenty-year anniversary.

The following are gift ideas and how they should be used.

Books

Few people in business don't appreciate books. Popular business books about how to build the bottom line, improve employee performance, improve personal performance, or make money in the stock market can be given to clients, vendors, employers, and employees. A book on someone's particular hobby is always appreciated.

Dinner Certificates

Everyone enjoys receiving dinner certificates. I still remember a business associate I did a favor for giving me a $300 gift certificate to Le Bec-Fin in Philadelphia—which many people consider the finest restaurant in America. That certificate was given to me ten years ago and my wife and I still talk about it. It's important when giving a gift certificate, however, that the amount covers two full dinners.

Giveaway Items

Giveaway items are great and people usually appreciate them. Coffee mugs, nice pens, letter openers are all fine, but you need to be creative. You don't have to spend a lot of money to be effective.

High-quality, well-designed or clever t-shirts are also appreciated. Eight years ago, I received a t-shirt from a company in Altoona, Pennsylvania, called New Pig. I still wear that t-shirt.

friend who runs a financial printing business gives beautiful, unique gifts. Instead of pens and calendars he gives potholders, yo-yos, and children's books written by a former employee. People rave about the variety, fun, and usefulness of his gifts.

Tickets to Events

Like dinner, everyone appreciates being invited somewhere. It doesn't matter what type of event, although the more prestigious the event the longer the memory of the person receiving the tickets. One business associate of mine treated my father and me to the baseball playoffs and the World Series. You can bet I never forgot their kindness.

When giving a gift, don't expect a return on investment or even a thank-you. Remember that you sent that gift because you are thanking that person for doing something special.

Hosting Business Associates at Home

Hosting business associates at your home can develop relationships that last a lifetime. Most of my closest friends are people I have met through business. What has made our relationships grow has been our social interaction. You need to be able to talk about more than business to develop a strong bond.

When hosting people at your home, you want them to feel comfortable. Tell your guests to dress casually and ask them what they like to eat. Many times people prepare for their guests as if they were hosting the president of the United States. Don't go overboard when making a meal; you don't want to become so stressed out that you can't enjoy your company.

I can assure you your guest is just as concerned as you are about making the right impression. Take the anxiety out of the evening for both you and your guest. Send your guest typed directions to your home that include your telephone number. Ask him or her to arrive around 5 P.M. and serve dinner between 6:00 and 6:30 P.M. If there are children, serve the children first and have toys or activities available for them in a separate area so you can have meaningful conversation.

Serve appetizers that aren't messy and offer beer and soft drinks. Dinner should be something that isn't messy to eat, so your guests aren't afraid of appearing to be sloppy. Dessert can be something simple like a cheesecake served with a fresh pot of coffee.

Many people who invite business associates over for dinner make a concerted effort to stay away from discussing business because they don't want to appear to be one-dimensional and want to respect the guest's possible desire to leave business at the office. I see nothing wrong with starting the conversation by mentioning business, however, because that is a topic your guest will initially be comfortable with. The trick is to get beyond that.

Stay away from topics such as politics and religion until you get to know your guest well. It's best to discuss vacations, sports, children, and homes—all topics people usually are comfortable with and have opinions about.

Inviting Business Associates to Events

Everyone likes some type of event, whether it be a sporting event, the theater, the ballet, or a new exhibit at the art museum. Find out what your business associates enjoy and get tickets for them. Don't just give the person two tickets—accompany your guests so you will get to know them. Going to an event your associate enjoys will add to the experiences you have in common. The more you have in common, the closer your relationship will become and the more business you will do together.

Finally, whether it be dinner or an event, don't forget to prepare your spouse or significant other about your guests and what are good and bad topics for conversation. I remember having dinner at a friend's when my friend's wife made an unflattering comment about another businessperson. One of the guests was good friends with that person, and it made for an awkward evening.

Finally, I can't overstate how important maintaining and cultivating relationships are for long-term success. Having a college degree, or even an advanced degree, is no longer insurance against unemployment. It is rare that someone lands an opportunity, outside of a specialized field such as computer programming, without knowing someone or someone who knows someone else.

Business has become so competitive and technology changes so quickly that few companies have a distinct advantage over others. It's personal relationships that ultimately decide whether you get a sale or keep an account. Never forget that and you will prosper.

7

Networking at Different Corporate Levels

Many people are under the assumption that if you want to get a job or make a deal, you need to know and talk to the president of the company. In companies with less than 50 people that probably is true because decision making is centralized and the owner or president probably controls the purse strings for hiring and buying. In medium-sized and large companies, however, the president is usually only involved in hiring people who directly report to him or her and in making large capital purchase decisions. Ninety percent of the decisions are made by departmental executives and line managers. These people are in charge of the budget process, have profit-and-loss responsibility, and are given the freedom to make decisions.

Companies of more than 50 people can't move forward and be successful if one or two individuals are making all of the decisions. Other people have to be given authority to develop a strong chain of command. The trick to being a successful networker is knowing who are the right people to contact and what power they wield in a company.

Choosing Appropriate Contacts

Companies of 50 to 100 employees or more usually have the following departments:

- Finance
- Human resources
- Manufacturing
- Management information systems
- Marketing/public relations
- Research and development
- Sales

Each of these companies, depending on the size of the business, has a management tree similar to the one shown in Figure 7.1. Some companies go deeper and some are flatter. Some have separate groups for customer service and legal services and others don't. The flow chart shown gives you an idea of all the people who have the ability to hire and buy goods and services.

It isn't easy to determine who you should contact in an organization to get business or a position. If you don't know anything about an organization's internal structure, the best thing to do is write to the president and her office will send your letter to the appropriate person. The president's office usually sends a letter, or calls the inquiring person, with the appropriate organizational contact.

In the event that you can get your hands on a company's organizational chart, write to the appropriate executive vice president regarding your interest in the company. Your letter will either be answered by that person or will flow down the chain of command to the appropriate person, who will answer the letter because it came from the boss (or the boss's boss).

If you are looking for employment, never write to the head of human resources. It has been my experience that organizations aren't clear in communication to their human resources departments on what exactly they are looking for. You have a better chance by writing to the executive in charge of your area of interest.

Finding Information About Potential Contacts

Before meeting someone, it's good to know something about the person you are meeting and the company he or she works

Figure 7.1 Management Chart for a Large Company

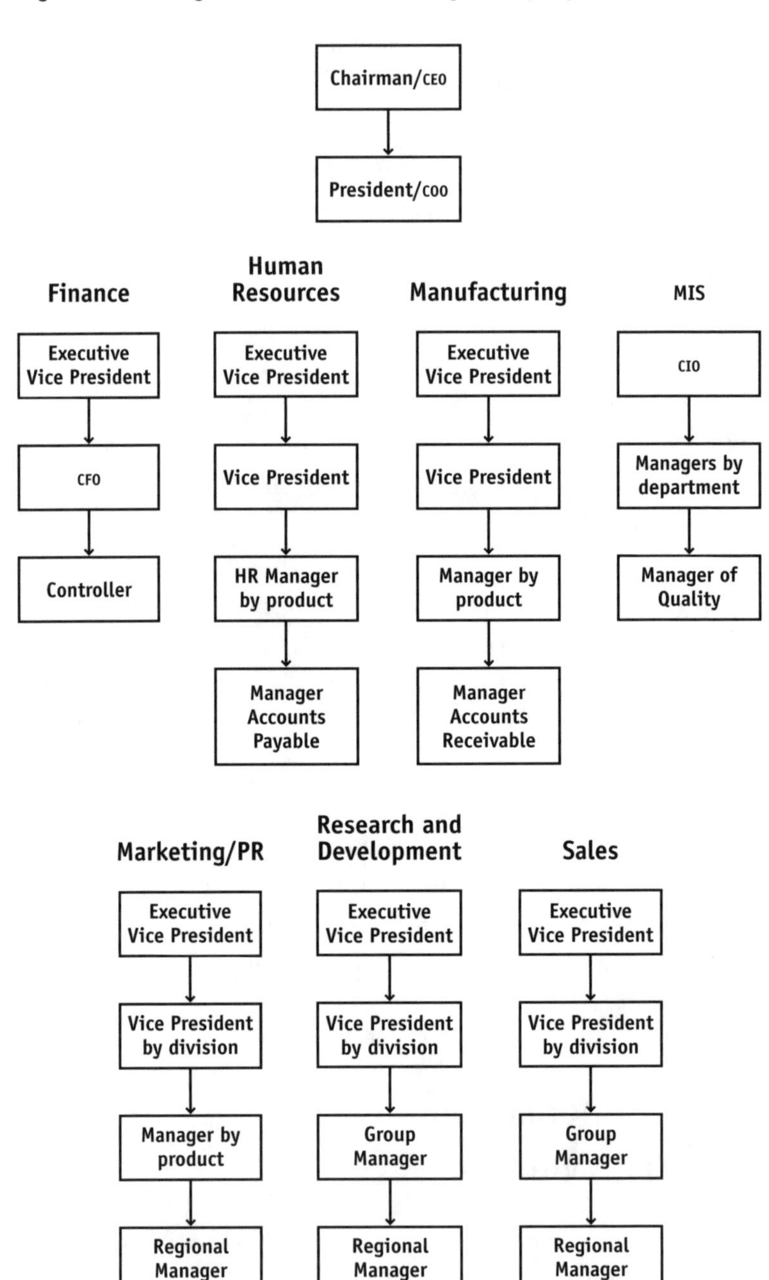

for. Depending on the person's level within the organization, it is sometimes hard to find out any more than the person's title. There are a variety of sources you can use to find out more about the person and the company.

Internet and Other Database Searches

Go on the Internet and use a search engine such as AltaVista (www.altavista.com), Infoseek (www.Infoseek.com), Lycos (www.lycos.com), or Yahoo (www.yahoo.com), which are free, or Electric Library (www.elibrary.com), which is a fee-based service.

AltaVista and Yahoo will allow you to look up a company's or person's name and see if anything has been written about that organization or individual. These two search engines are best used for finding information on a particular company, as opposed to an individual.

Electric Library helps you find information on both individuals and companies. This search engine scans hundreds of periodicals from the *New York Times* to the *Philadelphia Business Journal.* The people you are most likely to find when doing a search on Electric Library are the top executives of the company, such as the chairman, president/CEO, chief financial officer, and the vice presidents of sales, marketing, human resources, and information systems. These people are usually quoted in trade journals and regional publications in stories on something related to the person's position in a company.

Every day more trade journals and regional publications can be found to have an Internet presence. These publications are a great source of information during an Internet search.

Most college, university, and large city and county libraries also have database systems that allow you to find articles on people and companies that may not be available on the Internet. The librarian can help you to search these systems.

The Company Itself

You can also get information on a large company from the company itself. You can, for example, send for the company's promotional material and newsletter. There is a wealth of information in a company newsletter. For public companies, call the company's investor relations department and ask for the annual report and press releases. You can also call a stockbroker and ask him or her to send you a research report on the company.

Trade Associations, Industry Research Firms, and Chambers of Commerce

Information on a company can also be obtained from industry organizations. One source is the trade association to which the person and company belong. Another source is industry research firms such as Dataquest, who follow many different industries and issue reports on those industries. The reports talk about specific companies and the individuals who run those companies. You can also get valuable information from chamber of commerce membership directories. These directories usually have descriptions of their organizational members and the names of the top executives.

Networking for Sales with Everyone Below the Top Executive Offices

The bulk of a corporation's budget is controlled by people below the rank of vice president in most companies. That will surprise many reading this book, but it's true. Companies create lots of small- to medium-sized pots of money for managers throughout an organization to spend.

When dealing with people below the executive offices, you have to realize that no matter how much the president says he or she wants the company's people to feel empowered, to take risks and not feel they will be fired for making mistakes, most managers are afraid their decisions will get them fired. They want constant reassurance that they are making the right decision. When they buy your product or service, they feel they are putting their careers in your hands.

Ask your customers what you can do to make them shine. I have, for example, written glowing letters to bosses of the people who have hired my company to do work. Anyone about whom you have written a positive letter will go out of his or her way to make sure you get additional work and help you navigate through corporate politics. It can be very beneficial to write your customer a nice letter thanking him or her for the work he or she did or for the opportunity to work with his or her company. Letter 7.1 is a letter I wrote for one customer.

Networking with Company Presidents

There are three things you should keep in mind when dealing with a president of a company: the size of his or her ego, professional time constraints, and whether what you have to say provides him or her with any significant value. Presidents are looking for solutions to problems or ways to increase income.

The size of the company and the president's stature in the business community should dictate how you interact with him

Thank-You Letter to a Customer

Ms. Mary Smith
Marketing Manager
Jones Corporation
55 Jones Court
Jonesville, PA 19555

Dear Mary:

Thank you for the opportunity to work with your company. You were a pleasure to work with. I don't think the project would have been as successful if we didn't have your input and encouragement.

I will call you to set up a lunch to review the project and see what areas we can improve in the future. We want to make sure we do a great job of servicing your company's needs. I will call you within the next few days to pick a date.

Sincerely,

Marc Kramer
Project Manager

or her. I believe in treating everyone the same, regardless of size of company, but unfortunately that doesn't always work.

Some company presidents have large egos. Usually, the larger the company, the greater the ego. The reason is that these people wield immense power, sit on the most prestigious for-profit and nonprofit boards, and are treated like rock stars. Few people dare tell them they are wrong, and after a period of time they may begin to believe they are infallible.

There are times you will be in a position to speak with a president of a company you want to do business with. You might meet him or her at a charity function or an industry event. Realizing there are a lot of people who want the president's time and business, you need to work fast. The following are sample conversations that may move your agenda forward.

Example 1

YOU: Mr. Jones, my name is Marc Kramer. I am with Mixed Media Works, and we develop internal and external websites. I noticed that your company doesn't have a presence on the World Wide Web, and I would like to know who to speak to in your organization.

MR. JONES: When you say you do Web development, what does that mean?

YOU: We develop the graphics and the content. It's kind of like developing a television show. The person we typically interact with in a company is the vice president of marketing for external sites, and the CIO or head of human resources for internal websites.

Mr. Jones: I understand. You need to speak with Dawn Taggert. She is director of marketing and is in charge of the website task force.

You: May I have your business card, so I can write her name on the back? Also, would you mind if I said you suggested I give her a call?

Mr. Jones: I don't mind. Here is my card.

You: Thank you.

Example 2

You: Mr. Jones, my name is Marc Kramer and I am with Mixed Media Works. We develop websites. I am very impressed with your products and I was wondering why you don't have a website?

Mr. Jones: We are thinking about putting one together.

You: May I have your business card? Who should I speak with in your organization?

In both examples, we didn't take up much of Mr. Jones's time, and we got directly to the point on both occasions. The last thing Mr. Jones wants is for you to try to sell him something on the spot.

I have been very fortunate in my interaction with CEOs and have gotten a lot of business from them. When I was running the Penn State Technology Development Center, a business incubator for start-up technology companies, I wrote to major regional CEOs and tried to get them to visit the incubator to address my tenants. The purpose was for these CEOs to impart their wisdom about building a successful business and to open up opportunities for my tenants to do business with their companies.

One day, the CEO of one of the most well-known and successful start-ups in the Philadelphia region called me personally. He told me I had 60 seconds to make a case for why he should take time out of his day to speak to my tenants. I told him that no one in the state had built a better company faster than he, his office was less than a mile from the incubator so he could make his speech on his way home, and that most of my tenants had requested we get him as a speaker. He then asked me what day I wanted him.

The preceding example underscores the need to be prepared to state your case convincingly, yet concisely when the opportunity arises. It is also important to make it as easy as possible for the person to respond to your request. For example, always, if you have the flexibility, allow the person to choose the date for a meeting or other event, or have multiple dates for him or her to choose from. If you offer only one date and it doesn't fit his or her calendar, the person will be forced to decline.

Networking with Second-Tier Executives

My definition of second-tier executives is executives who report to the people who report to the president. These are department and divisional managers and vice presidents. They are people who have line responsibility, which means they control budgets.

In many cases, second-tier executives are aspiring future presidents who believe they have the ability to run an organization, but are careful not to offend or take unnecessary risks with someone higher up, major suppliers, or peers. They are people who will usually take the time to learn more about you and your organization, because whether they make a good or bad selection could impact their career.

If you make such an executive look good and his or her career advances, you can expect additional business. On the other hand, if you let the executive down, he or she probably won't do business with you in the future. When dealing with second-tier executives, find out what their goals are and how you can play a role in helping them achieve them.

Many second-tier executives go to trade shows and a few even are involved on the boards of regional nonprofits. The best place to find these people is trade shows or events where their bosses are being honored. Unlike presidents, whose pictures you have seen in publications, annual reports, and the like, you probably won't know these people by sight. You will have to look at their name tags and hope they will be helpful. Below are examples of how to develop relationships with second-tier executives.

Example 1

YOU: Hi, my name is Marc Kramer and I'm with Mixed Media Works. I see you are with Jones Aerospace. Your company makes parts for space shuttles, right?

MS. DUNCAN: That's right!

YOU: What do you do for Jones Aerospace?

MS. DUNCAN: I am a group manager in the MIS department. I oversee a group of programmers that develop software for testing our parts.

YOU: How many employees are in your company?

MS. DUNCAN: Oh, about 900. Most are in our home office in Alexandria, Virginia.

YOU: Does your company have a website?

MS. DUNCAN: No! I understand we are thinking of developing one.

YOU: My company develops corporate Internet and intranet sites. We would be interested in speaking with whoever is in charge of the project. Can you connect me with the person in charge or give me his or her name to write or call?

MS. DUNCAN: Give me your card and I will see it gets to the right person.

YOU: I would appreciate it. It might be just as easy if I contacted the person myself rather than bother you.

MS. DUNCAN: No bother!

YOU: Please give me your card and I will call you later in the week to see what the next step is. I will send you a packet of information on us when I get back to the office. Thanks a lot for your help.

Example 2

YOU: I see you work for Jones Corp. How are things going there?

MR. COTE: Not bad. My division is doing well.

YOU: My name's Marc Kramer. I'm a sales manager for a multimedia company called Mixed Media Works. We are an outsourcer for developing and maintaining Internet and intranet websites. What do you do for Jones Corp.?

MR. COTE: My name's John Cote and I am a marketing strategist for the telecommunications group.

YOU: What do you do exactly?

MR. COTE: We sell computer hardware and software solutions to telephone companies. We help them develop billing and collection tracking systems. Right now, we provide 60 percent of the world's telephone companies with these types of systems.

YOU: My company has been interested in partnering with Jones and doing work for Jones for a long time. Our company's headquarters is only three miles from Jones's headquarters. Who would I speak with in regards to possibly forming a partnership? We could do the creative end and content management, while Jones provides the back-end solution.

MR. COTE: Your timing is actually good. Part of my job is to identify Web development companies who do what you do and to contract out developing a website for our division.

YOU: Great! I don't want to take up any more of your time. How about if I call you tomorrow to set up an appointment?

MR. COTE: Here is my card, which has my e-mail address. Why don't you give me a few dates that work for you and we will set up a time.

YOU: Thanks. I look forward to seeing you.

As soon as you get back to the office, make sure you write. People have short memories, so it is imperative you follow up with a letter and telephone call within three to five days of meeting someone. (See Chapter 5 for advice on how to write a good follow-up letter.)

The most important thing to remember in maintaining your networking relationships is following up with people you've met by providing them with information about yourself and your company, or by carrying out a promise you made. I often offer people whose business I want an introduction to someone in my network they would like to do business with. I always make sure to follow up with both a note and a telephone call to make the connection, and then follow up with another call to see if the connection worked. This gives me numerous opportunities to develop a relationship with my new contact.

8

Good Networking Organizations

In Chapter 2, "Networking to Find the Right Job," I wrote about the types of organizations in which you could find quality contacts. In this chapter, I provide information on how to contact some of those organizations to get your network started. Locating good networking organizations is one of the first steps in forming a vital network.

Chambers of commerce and large regional Boy Scout troops should be easy to find in a telephone book. Your local chamber of commerce and your state's department of commerce will be able to help you find some organizations in your region and state.

There are many ways to determine which organizations provide the best networking opportunities. Look at the regional weekly business newspaper or magazine and see which organizations have the most seminars. Talk to friends and colleagues and find out what organizations they belong to, who attends their meetings, and if these contacts have lead to new business. I've also included some examples of how networking with different organizations has helped me.

Public Organizations

Public entities are funded by both taxpayer dollars and private sector dollars. They provide capital to entrepreneurial and manufacturing businesses for creating jobs. These organizations attract high level executives and venture capitalists to their boards and committees, who then determine how to distribute capital or support from the organization. These individuals are looking for experienced professionals, as well as capital.

Business Incubators

Like county industrial development authorities, many counties and cities have business incubators that provide inexpensive office space, shared secretarial services, other office amenities, and business advisory assistance. These groups run business card exchanges and seminars that allow tenants to meet businesspeople both within and outside the incubator. For a list of business incubators around the country, contact the National Business Incubator Association, 20 E. Circle Drive, Suite 190, Athens, OH 45701.

During my time running the Eastern Technology Council, I interacted often with different executive directors of industrial development authorities (IDAS) who were trying to help out-of-state companies find a suitable location in their counties. I struck up a friendship with these people because I knew that if I could help them land a company, I would enhance my chances of getting a new member. I offered to introduce local presidents of similar industries to any prospect they brought to the region. Because of this relationship, my organization landed some very large regional companies as members.

One of them was British Technology Group, the world's largest privately held technology transfer company. Through the executive directors of one of the county IDAS, I met Dr. Derek Schafer, who was president of the American subsidiary. Within six months, Dr. Schafer joined the Technology Council, became a board member, and two years later helped me start the Pennsylvania Technology Transfer Center.

County Industrial Development Authorities

Many counties have economic development organizations that promote a particular region by providing loans, grants, and other financial and service inducements to lure business to an area. These organizations, which usually carry the name of the county or city they serve, have monthly business card

I started the Penn State Technology Development Center, which no longer exists but in the late 1980s was one of the top business incubators in the United States. During my tenure as manager of the center, one of my tenants' employees was a computer programmer named Bill Schnell. Bill was and is a very bright guy and talked about leaving his employer to start his own consulting business. After I left the center, I didn't see Bill for a few years, during which time he did start his own company and joined the trade association I was running. One day we had lunch and he told me he needed someone to help him think through the issues of growing his business. He then asked me if I would be interested in consulting with him and I accepted.

exchanges. Look for the names of these groups in your telephone book or call the county commissioner's or mayor's office in your area.

Small Business Development Centers

SBDCs can be found in practically every state in the United States. These semipublic organizations are usually connected with universities and provide business assistance to entrepreneurs. SBDCs, which are funded by federal and state government, run seminars for entrepreneurs on marketing, finance, sales, and hiring. Contact your state department of commerce or the largest university business school in your state to find out about this organization.

Government Entities

Government entities are funded by taxpayer dollars to provide capital for business growth and to increase employment opportunities. The government entities listed here are examples from Pennsylvania. Pennsylvania, because of its dying manufacturing base, became a leader in developing entities to support business creation. Contact your state's department of commerce, which is in your local telephone book, or call your county industrial development authority to find similar organizations. The local state and federal legislative offices will be familiar with these entities, as will bank loan officers that concentrate on business lending. The best source to find what each state, and many counties, has to offer is the National Business Incubation Association, 20 E. Circle Drive, Suite 190, Athens, OH 45701.

Ben Franklin Technology Center. BFTC was created in the early 1980s to provide venture and working capital for technology and manufacturing start-up companies in Pennsylvania. BFTC has four offices around the state, but the main office is in Harrisburg. For more information, contact Ben Franklin Partnership, c/o Department of Commerce, 471 Forum Building, Harrisburg, PA 17120; webmaster@state.paus.com.

Delaware Valley Industrial Resource Center. DVIRC, which is located outside of Philadelphia, was developed by Governor Robert Casey in the late 1980s to support the greater Philadelphia manufacturing base. The organization has evolved into a great place for manufacturers of all sizes to network and share ideas. Contact Delaware Valley Industrial Resource Center, 12265 Townsend Road, Philadelphia, PA 19154.

Private Nonprofit Organizations

Private nonprofit organizations are created and funded by private sector companies to fulfill a need, whether in business education, capital formation, or job creation. These organizations mirror public ones in terms of who sits on their boards and committees and who contacts them for investment and assistance. The difference is that this group involves presidents of mid-sized to large companies. They join to network with their peers and because they feel an obligation to make a difference in society, apart from making money. Following is a sample of private nonprofit organizations.

Association for Corporate Growth. This organization brings the top executives of mid-sized to large public companies together to talk about buying, selling, and financing businesses. Contact Association for Corporate Growth, 2 Penn Center Plaza, Philadelphia, PA 19102.

The Capital Network. One of the premier angel networks in the United States. Located at the University of Texas, this organization brings its investor members together with entrepreneurs looking for capital. Contact David Gerhardt, 3925 W. Braker Lane, Suite 406, Austin, TX 78759; tcn@ati.utexas.edu.

Center for Entrepreneurial Management. This is the world's largest nonprofit membership association of entrepreneurs and CEOs. Contact Center for Entrepreneurial Management, 18 Varick Street, New York, NY 10014; www.ceo/clubs.org.

Executive Network. This organization brings presidents and owners of businesses together to share ideas, experiences, and solutions to current industry problems with other noncompetitors. Contact Executive Network, 9300 Shelbyville Road, Suite 1020, Louisville, KY 40222.

The Investors Circle. The members of this organization come from all over the country and invest in entrepreneurial activities that are socially responsible. Contact The Investors Circle, 3220 Sacramento Street, San Francisco, CA 94115.

Pacific Northwest Capital Network. This organization assists entrepreneurs in the state of Washington to find investors. Contact the Pacific Northwest Capital Network, 4015 181 Avenue SE, Bellevue, WA 98008.

Pennsylvania Private Investors Group. PPIG is a group of investor angels who meet on a monthly basis to listen to and possibly invest in entrepreneurs who are looking for investors. (An investor angel is an accredited investor with $250,000 in disposable income or a net worth of $1 million who invests in entrepreneurial businesses.) Over the past five years, 13 companies have received almost $20 million in investment capital. Contact Pennsylvania Private Investors Group, 3624 W. Market Street, Philadelphia, PA 19107; esissel@bftc.libertynet.org.

Technology Capital Network at MIT. This organization was the successor of the first investor angels network, called the New Hampshire Capital Network. TCN brings together entrepre-

In November of 1996, I was in the elevator of the Marriott in downtown Philadelphia going to the fifth annual Enterprise Awards, which I had started when I ran the Eastern Technology Council. Only this time I was coming as a guest like everyone else. In the elevator ride to the reception before the event, I met the CEO of MedQuist, Inc., who was a finalist for one of the awards. MedQuist provides business and information services to hospitals and other health care providers.

During our 60-second ride up in the elevator, I asked him if he was going to the Enterprise Awards and he told me he was a finalist. I asked him if his company had a website because I was president of a company that specialized in developing websites for Fortune 1000 companies. We exchanged business cards and I followed up the next day with a faxed memo that restated what my company does and who in my organization would call his office. The result of this was two contracts.

neurs and investors from the New England region of the country. Contact Technology Capital Network, 290 Main Street, Lower Level, Cambridge, MA 02139.

World Affairs Council. There are chapters of this organization throughout the United States. WAC hosts events that feature business, political, and entertainment leaders. What makes this organization attractive from a networking standpoint is the people it attracts, who are top executives from many different fields. Its annual dinner provides a great opportunity to find new business and new employment opportunities. Contact World Affairs Council, 1314 Chestnut Street, Philadelphia, PA 19107; wac@libertynet.org.

Events

Events are created to bring visibility to organizations while increasing participation and to bring together key players to encourage business opportunities. Contact the office of the person heading the event and ask for a list of chair- and co-chairpeople. This will provide you insight on the magnitude of the event and quality of the people attending. Also consider contacting your local libraries and museums for a schedule of their major events, which are often attended by business leaders. The following events are examples from the eastern United States.

Borrowers Ball. The Philadelphia Library, like many big city libraries around the country, runs an annual fund-raising event. This event is comprised of an auction, black-tie dinner, and dancing. All of the elite of the Philadelphia region attend this event.

Eastern Technology Council's Enterprise Awards. The Eastern Technology Council, which covers eastern Pennsylvania, southern New Jersey, and Delaware, runs one of the largest business technology awards dinners in the United States with more than 500 business moguls and their top lieutenants in attendance. Ten awards are given, and there are three finalists for each award. There is no better place to speak with the movers and shakers of the greater Philadelphia technology community than this event.

Ernst & Young/Inc. Magazine Entrepreneur of the Year Dinner. The premier national business award for entrepreneurs. This award is given out in every major city in the United States, and there is a national convention in Palm

In June of 1996, I attended the Philadelphia Entrepreneur of the Year dinner as a guest of the chairman of Global Financial Press, Phillip Kendall. I sat next to Irwin Gross, cofounder and chairman of Englehard-ICC, which makes air filter systems. I told him about my company and he put me in contact with his vice president of marketing, Richard Sweetser. After three meetings with Mr. Sweetser, we ended up with a Web development contract.

Springs every November. It's a great place to meet the best and brightest locally and nationally in business.

Greater Philadelphia Venture Group's Annual Awards. Most major cities have venture capital associations that bring together the region's professional and semiprofessional venture capitalists. Contact Greater Philadelphia Venture Group, 200 S. Broad Street, Suite 700, Philadelphia, PA 19102-3896.

MidAtlantic Venture Capital Fair. This event is a forum for entrepreneurial companies to raise capital from institutional and corporate venture capitalists and private investors. It is brought together by the Greater Philadelphia Venture Group and the Baltimore Venture Capital Group. Contact Greater Philadelphia Venture Group, 200 S. Broad Street, Suite 700, Philadelphia, PA 19102-3896.

New Jersey Technology Council Awards. New Jersey's top event for bringing together the business and academic leaders of the technology community. Contact New Jersey Technical Council Awards, 500 College Road East, Suite 201, Princeton, NJ 08540.

Political Fund-Raisers. Political dinners that raise money for state and federal senators and representatives, mayors of all sizes of cities, and county commissioners attract high-level businesspeople from all fields. Attendees are the people who are targeted to give, have the most to gain by giving, and have the financial wherewithal to give.

Walnut Street Theater Annual Dinner. The Walnut Street Theater is the oldest major theater in the United States and every year it honors someone from the Philadelphia region business community that supports theater. This dinner is attended by presidents of companies and partners in major service firms. Similar events are sponsored by arts organizations in other major cities.

Trade Associations

Trade associations enable companies to buy and sell products and services to each other and to educate their members, the public at large, and government officials at the local, county, state, and federal levels. Almost every field has trade associations. You can find these organizations through *The Encyclopedia of Associations* (Gale Research) and *National Trade and Professional Associations* (Columbia Books), which can be found in most libraries.

These organizations are overseen by trustees that are top executives in the field. Some—depending on their prestige, size, uniqueness, or newness—attract presidents and other high level executives to their seminars and annual events. Some only attract people who are new to the industry, because those with experience in the field no longer benefit from attending the association's activities. It is my experience that technology councils and industries focused on technology products bring the best cross-section of quality contacts. The following list focuses on this part of the trade association arena.

American Electronics Association. AEA has chapters all over the world. It brings together the top executives of electronics companies to talk about common problems and plan lobbying for laws beneficial to electronics companies. Contact American Electronics Association, 1225 I Street NW, Suite 950, Washington, DC 20005.

Atlanta Women's Network. AWN brings together women business owners and executives to discuss issues affecting women in business and for networking to develop new business. Contact Atlanta Women's Network, P.O. Box 870434, Atlanta, GA 30347; willco@t-i-a.com.

Biotechnology Industry Organization. BIO is the premier organization bringing together biotechnology companies and universities that develop research for biotechnology companies. Contact Biotechnology Industry Organization, 1625 K Street NW, Suite 1100, Washington, DC 20006-1604.

The Electronic Commerce Association. This organization brings together business executives interested in buying and selling products through the Internet. Contact The Electronic Commerce Association, Ramillies House, 1-9 Hills Place, London W1R 1AG, England; eca@org.uk.

The Forum of Private Business. This organization brings together 22,000 business executives in Scotland and England to discuss making their countries more competitive internationally. Contact The Forum of Private Business, Drum Lane, Knutsford, Cheshire, England WA16 6HA.

International Franchise Association. This is the preeminent organization for people interested in buying or working with a franchise. These franchise developers and owners look for quality people in management, marketing, sales, information systems, and telemarketing. Contact International Franchise Association, 1350 New York Avenue NW, Suite 900, Washington DC 20005.

Licensing Executives Society. This organization brings together corporate, university, and individual professionals to buy and sell technology. It's a great forum to find new technology in which to spawn a new company or meet individuals who are starting a new company. Contact Licensing Executives Society, 1800 Diagonal Road, Suite 280, Alexandria, VA 22314.

Below are some names and addresses of some well-known technology councils. These councils provide a forum for product and service companies to buy and sell to each other, to create entrepreneur opportunities, and to increase visibility of the region each council serves.

Association of Technology Business Councils. There are more than 50 technology councils in the United States that range in size from 100 to more than 1,400 members. These organizations bring technology entrepreneurs together to buy, sell, and license products to each other and to provide investment capital. They run seminars, a major awards dinner, technology transfer programs, and private investor groups. Contact Association of Technology Business Councils, 1953 Gallows Road, Suite 130, Vienna, VA 22182.

Central Pennsylvania Technology Council. CPTA brings together companies whose goal is to promote technology growth in Central Pennsylvania. Contact Central Pennsylvania Technology Council, 225 State Street, Suite 360, Harrisburg, PA 17101.

Eastern Technology Council. This organization brings together all sizes of technology companies, universities, and organizations that provide services to technology companies in southeastern Pennsylvania. ETC runs more than 50 seminars a year that are both educational and provide great opportunities to meet executives. Contact Eastern Technology Council, 435 Devon Park Drive, Building 300, Wayne, PA 19087-1945; www.techcouncil.org.

Michigan Technology Council. This organization brings together executives from technology companies, universities, and companies that serve technology companies. Contact Michigan Technology Council, 2005 Baits Drive, Ann Arbor, MI 48109.

New Jersey Technology Council. NJTC brings together business and academic leaders of the technology community to buy, sell, and license technology products and services. Contact New Jersey Technology Council, 500 College Road East, Suite 201, Princeton, NJ 08540.

Northern Virginia Technology Council. Brings together business, government, and academic leaders to promote technology development. Contact Northern Virginia Technology Council, CTI Tower, Suite 601, 2214 Rock Hill Road, Herndon, VA 22070; rpelletr@clark.net.

Pittsburgh High Technology Council. The largest business technology council in the United States, PHTC hosts major trade shows, seminars, and awards dinners and is one of the most effective lobbying organizations in Pennsylvania for promoting technology development. Contact Pittsburgh High Technology Council, 4516 Henry Street, Pittsburgh, PA 15213.

Suburban Maryland High Technology Council. This organization is a close relative of the Northern Virginia Technology Council. Its primary purpose is to bring business, government, and academic leaders together to promote technology development in Maryland. Contact Suburban Maryland High Technology Council, 2092 Gaither Road, Suite 220 A, Rockeville, MD 20850; info@mdhtech.org.

There are no better places to find good networking opportunities than trade associations and major events run by socially responsible nonprofit organizations, such as those listed in this chapter. Some of the events and associations might appear financially expensive, but the potential contacts make the investment worth it.

9

Starting Your Own Networking Organization

A bold networking option few people consider is to start their own networking organization. Most people simply join an existing organization, but developing your own organization has great advantages, as the founders of the Eastern Technology Council found out.

Starting your own organization can be fun, and, more importantly, professionally rewarding. Starting an organization gives you visibility and a reason to contact someone who, under normal circumstances, might not be willing to take your telephone call. Opportunities you never conceived of can open up through the people you come in contact with and the initiatives your organization undertakes.

The first section of this chapter gives an example to demonstrate the value of starting your own organization. The second section gives advice on how to start a networking organization.

An Example: The Eastern Technology Council

In the fall of 1989, Dr. Hubert Schoemaker, chairman of Centocor, one of the world's foremost biotechnology companies, was asked by then Pennsylvania Governor Robert P. Casey to bring together a group of technology company presidents to discuss the possibility of starting an organization that served the technology business community. This organization, of which I would become the first executive director, was originally called the Technology Council of Greater Philadelphia. As it expanded, it became the Eastern Technology Council. The primary purpose of this organization is to bring together top executives of all sizes of companies to buy and sell products and services and to transfer technology.

During the time I ran this organization, from 1990 to 1995, members received benefits that exceeded their wildest expectations. Most of these people joined with the hope of finding new employees, a piece of technology that would advance their businesses, good strategic partners, and maybe leads on possible contracts. The following are examples of what a good networking organization can bring to those who decide to get involved in leading it.

In the first year of the organization's existence, Dr. Schoemaker and Mr. Warren V. Musser, legendary chairman of Safeguard Scientifics, a publicly traded company that invested in technology companies and eventually took them public, decided the Greater Philadelphia region needed a large seed-stage venture capital fund. With the help of J. P. Morgan, one of the world's premier investment banks, they started a $60 million venture capital fund called Technology Leaders. Mr. Musser's company managed the fund and many of the Technology Council board members sat on the board of the fund. These board members received equity in the fund worth millions of dollars. A second fund, managed by the same group, was started a few years later and to date almost 30 companies have received approximately $100 million in venture capital and more than 2,000 new jobs have been created.

Michael Emmi, chairman/CEO of Systems Computer Technology, a publicly traded NASDQ company, had few contacts when he came to the Philadelphia region in the late 1980s. Through his involvement in the ETC as a board member, Mr. Emmi was invited to be on the board of two public companies and got a multimillion-dollar contract from a large regional utility company.

George Gordon, one of the founding board members of the ETC, was chairman/CEO of a sizable electronics company in the Philadelphia region, but had decided to leave and buy another company. His new company, Datamatix, received more than $1 million from the new venture fund.

Dr. Derek Schafer, former president/CEO of British Technology Group USA, one of the leaders in technology transfer and commercialization, became a board member of ETC in the organization's first year. In my last year at ETC, Dr. Schafer and I codeveloped a new program, administrated by ETC, called the Pennsylvania Technology Transfer Center. Dr. Schafer, who by this time had a new company, received a contract to devise a strategy to transfer technology between Pennsylvania companies and entrepreneurs.

Mark Talaba was a vice president of a computer networking company and one of the first 20 members of the ETC. Mr. Talaba, through contacts at the ETC, was recommended to be president of a computer consulting firm. He is now president/CEO and part owner of the consulting firm Softwrite.

Tom Drury, president of Sensar, which developed Iris scanning technology used by banks to make sure a person using an automated teller machine card actually owns the card he or she is using, found the technology that became the foundation of his company through networking at Eastern Technology Council functions.

There are two examples of people who have benefited from the Eastern Technology Council that didn't start there. Molly Hoyle was a marketing director at Ernst & Young for ten years and helped launch the prestigious Entrepreneur of the Year awards. She didn't see a promising future at Ernst & Young and told me of her decision to leave. I had met partners at Price Waterhouse through starting the Eastern Technology

Council, and I made an introduction for her. Ms. Hoyle became director of marketing for Price Waterhouse in Philadelphia, which was thrilled to get someone of her experience.

John Kiely, a partner at Price Waterhouse, sponsored the Eastern Technology Council's electronics group from its inception. Through that sponsorship he acquired Elastomeric Technologies as a client.

There are more than a hundred other examples of how people benefited through their involvement with ETC. The reason ETC has been successful is because, like any successful business, the founders saw a need that wasn't being fulfilled and dedicated the organization to meeting that need.

How to Begin

Starting your own networking organization takes time, good organizational skills, and cooperation from other people.

Starting an association takes a great commitment of time and personal resources; it is no different than starting a for-profit business. For the first few years it takes seventy to 100 "people" hours per week.

This isn't just one person's time, because often it is impossible to get a single person to fully commit to starting an organization. If a few people believe in the organization and define up front how large the organization will be, and what type of activities it will involve itself in, that will determine the level of people involvement.

Organizations like the Pennsylvania Private Investors Group (an investor angels network that has 50 members and meets on a monthly basis) can be launched and run efficiently for $10,000 to $15,000. ETC, one of the largest business trade associations in the United States, was launched with $25,000, but its operating budget is now over $1 million. Pennsylvania Private Investors Group's target market was much smaller than ETC's, because there are fewer people who qualify as accredited investors, while anyone can join ETC.

Below is a brief ten-step outline to forming an organization.

1. Decide what type of organization you want to start, see if one exists in your region, and think about how you and others could benefit.
2. Develop a business plan. Building a successful organization is no different from developing a successful business. It is best to write a business plan and have others review it.
3. Make a list of possible members.
4. Make a list of possible activities and benefits members would receive.
5. Put together a board of directors. This board should have contacts with the type of people you are trying to recruit and experience in building organizations. Try to attract a respected name in the business community to be the chairperson.
6. Make a list of possible financial sponsors who would have an interest in underwriting your group's activities. Membership dues and event entrance fees may be sufficient, but most organizations need financial sponsors. Look for sponsors who would benefit by getting new business, raising their visibility, or giving the community a positive impression of themselves.
7. Have your board read and review your plan.
8. Hire an executive director to run the organization or outsource it to an association management company.

9. Develop a brochure you can distribute and put on the Internet outlining the activities and benefits of the organization.
10. Schedule a major kickoff event such as a breakfast or luncheon with a famous speaker. At this event, encourage people to fill out applications to join the organization.

The only way to keep the momentum going after an organization is launched is through dedicated leadership. In a small organization with no paid professional staff, the president and the board of directors are the driving force. With organizations like ETC, the president and executive director, who are full-time paid employees, have to eat, live, and breathe the organization.

Finally, networking organizations, like businesses, must constantly focus on staying fresh and generating new ideas. The reason the organization is successful today will probably not be the reason it is successful tomorrow. Listen to and provide your members with what they want and your organization will be successful. Think big and the rewards will be great. Just look at how the businesspeople who started the Eastern Technology Council benefited.

10

Networking Through the Internet

The newest frontier in technology is the explosion of the Internet. The Internet is the only forum in the world that isn't controlled by any one group and brings together people from all over the world. It's an unparalleled source of contacts and connections.

Like clubs and organizations, there is an Internet group for everyone. Right now, most of the chat groups and on-line services that bring people together are national and international. Few are local as I write this book, but that will probably change. America Online and Microsoft Network are developing regional networks, which will include local chat groups. There will be significant growth in on-line discussion through new products like WebTV that allow you to surf the net through your television in the comfort of your den.

Once many people have Internet access through their television sets, local services will become more robust and networking over the Internet will improve dramatically. The irony of the Internet is that instead of building regionally, which is how most products are rolled out, the Internet went national first and now is developing a local presence.

Once you are hooked up to the Internet, the best way to find chat rooms and on-line services is through search engines such as Alta Vista and Yahoo. Most regional newspapers and business magazines list business-related websites. You could start your own chat room or on-line service by working with a local Internet provider.

Chat Groups

There are innumerable chat rooms that cover just about every topic. If you have never participated in a chat group before or would like a comprehensive list of chat groups, check out the site at www.cloudnet.com/~ckcj/chat.htm. I haven't found most chat rooms to be helpful in terms of business networking, however, although many people do find them fun and educational when related to hobbies and medical issues. The following sections describe various chat rooms and services for cybernetworking to find employment, investment capital, and business advice. One helpful chat room, where a variety of business topics are discussed, is sponsored by *Entrepreneur Magazine*, one of the premier magazines geared toward small business owners and aspiring entrepreneurs, at www.entrepreneurmag.com.

On-Line Services

The following on-line services focus on helping people develop their business acumen, raise capital, and become entrepreneurs. Some not only provide good source material, but also contain leads to organizations that provide good networking opportunities.

Becoming an Entrepreneur

American Institute of Small Business. This organization creates educational materials aimed at helping people start their own businesses. The material isn't available at this site, but you can get information about ordering it.

Black Enterprise Online. This site is full of terrific tips and techniques that focus on helping black entrepreneurs. Website: www.blackenterprise.com.

Business Opportunities Handbook. This on-line magazine features articles about running a small business and marketing your products. It's almost like having free business consultants. Website: www.ezines.com.

The Entrepreneur Network. TEN is a nonprofit corporation dedicated to helping Midwest inventors and entrepreneurs through information and connections. Website: bizserve.com.

Entrepreneurial Edge Online. This site provides content on starting and growing a business, but more important for networkers, it provides seminar opportunities and links to other sites that also list seminar and conference opportunities. Website: www.edgeonline.com.

Ideas Digest Centre for Business. This site, which is run out of Vancouver, British Columbia, is focused on innovation and invention. There are employment and production acquisition opportunities. Website: www.rimart.com.

The Small Business Advisor. This website assists both start-ups and established companies. In particular, you can get help dealing with the federal government. It also has tips for entrepreneurs, links to other Internet resources, and gives information about ordering the organization's services. Website: www.isquare.com.

Employment Opportunities

According to AltaVista, one of the top search engines on the Internet, there are more than 90,000 employment opportunity related sites. Practically every major regional newspaper provides an on-line employment opportunity service. Below are some sites to get you started.

Career Magazine. This website is a comprehensive resource center featuring job openings, employer profiles, resumes, a directory of executive recruiters, and articles on finding a position. Website: www.careermag.com/classifieds/recruiters.

CareerPath. This site lists more than 100,000 employment opportunities culled from major newspapers from across the country. It is updated on a daily basis and allows the user to do keyword searches. Website: cpwebmaster@careerpath.com.

Executive BioSearch. This site links job seekers to other sites offering people in the sciences opportunities. Most of the opportunities are in the pharmaceutical and biopharmaceutical fields. Website: mail@healthcarejobs.com.

Infoseek. This is one of the top search engines on the Internet. You can go to Infoseek's business directory and click on the subheading for "Find a Job." This provides the following links: classifieds, career placement, job fairs, job hunting, job listings, posting your resume, resume banks, and resume services. Website: infoseek.com.

The Riley Guide. This site provides employment opportunities and job sources. Website: www.jobtrak.com/jobguide.

Raising Capital

The number of websites related to raising capital is growing every day. I have mentioned some of these sites in past chapters; below are some additional sites. Most entrepreneurs would agree that there isn't enough venture capital around for everyone, so more sites and investors are welcome. It's too early to tell which sites provide the best results.

I would suggest contacting the better business bureau in the town the company sponsoring the website is located in to make sure they are legitimate before using the site. Also ask for references or contact companies listed in the site for their comments.

Capital Matchmaker. This is one of the many stops on the Internet where an entrepreneurial company can present its company to investors. Website: www.matchmaker.org/capital/.

Finance Hub. Investors and entrepreneurs both have to pay for the privilege of participating in this site. The database of investors is in the thousands and there are links to dozens of venture capital firms. Website: www.financehub.com/vc/vctab.

International Capital Resources. This private company's mission is to help start-up companies raise money from private and institutional investors. It has a comprehensive database of contacts, produces a newsletter aimed at entrepreneurs in search of capital, and provides consulting services to advise start-ups on the process of raising capital. Website: www.icrnet.com. E-mail contact: jab@icrnet.com.

Women Incorporated. This website, targeted at women, provides a list of investor angel networks from around the country. At the writing of this book, there isn't a better site on the Internet for finding a comprehensive list of investor angel networks. It also provides expert advice on how to build a business and raise money. Website: www.capcon.com/worldfinance.

I believe the sites I have suggested are substantive and will improve over time. In the future you will see short video clips about the companies looking to raise money, the jobs companies are looking to fill, and what types of joint venture partners executives are looking for.

The Internet is constantly changing; many new sites will be up by the time you read this book. To keep up with the changes I suggest reading *Success* and *Inc.* and visiting their websites for links to other good business and employment websites. I believe you will see more major cities develop private investor groups, which will in turn have websites, to remain competitive in luring entrepreneurs to their regions.

Postscript

I hope you have found this book to be a quick and informative read. With the world shrinking because of technology, and with competition coming from all parts of the globe, having a college degree isn't enough to guarantee employment and success in business. Your greatest asset is your network of contacts and knowledge of your industry.

If you have questions, please write to me via e-mail at mkramer@p3.net.